Let There Be Light

Let There Be Light

Praying with Genesis

Revised Edition

ANGELA TILBY

DARTON · LONGMAN + TODD

First published in 1989 by
Darton, Longman and Todd Ltd
1 Spencer Court
140–142 Wandsworth High Street
London SW18 4JJ

This revised edition 2006

ISBN 0 232 52673 7

Phototypeset by
YHT Ltd, London
Printed and bound in Great Britain by
The Cromwell Press, Trowbridge, Wiltshire

In memory of my mother and father

Contents

Acknowledgements

Biblical quotations are taken from the New Revised Standard version of the Bible unless otherwise stated.

Andrei Rublev, *The Trinity*. See p. 92.
(Tretiakov Gallery, Moscow)

Pablo Picasso, *The Tragedy*. See p. 94.
(National Gallery of Art, Washington; Chester Dale Collection)

Introduction

Let There Be Light takes the form of seven meditations on the creation narrative of Genesis 1–2:3. It uses the text as a starting point for developing the life of prayer. One of the basic assumptions of this book is that God meets us as *persons*. You are the best authority on the way you need to pray, because God meets you as you are, on your own ground and within the pattern of your own personal history. So my aim has been to hint at how we might get in touch with our own ground and our own history and discover in them the work of the Creator God of Genesis. Each chapter concludes with a summary and seven suggestions for ways of praying. The variety is there to suit different needs and temperaments.

The format makes them suitable for use by individuals or groups as a Lent course. You could try using a chapter a week, starting in the week which includes Ash Wednesday.

The context

The material of this book originated as seven retreat addresses given to clergy at the House of the Resurrection, Mirfield. As these were delivered informally and from notes there are inevitably some expansions and contractions. It may help the reader to know that I was trying to make contact with the intellectual, emotional and spiritual issues which face ordained ministers in today's church. I think that these issues, whether we are aware of them or not, very deeply influence the way all Christian people in our society find themselves believing and praying.

Separations and beginnings

The creation narrative in Genesis 1–2:3 divides itself conveniently into seven parts. Seven days of creation provided seven retreat addresses, and have now become seven chapters!

I chose to use the Genesis text not only because it has always been a key text in our understanding of God's ways in the universe, but because it has spoken to me powerfully of the pattern of God's creative work in my own life. I have always found major life changes difficult. There have been two particularly hard transitions in my life so far, the breakdown of my marriage and the change of direction when I left the world of broadcasting to become an Anglican priest. During these painful periods I found the creation narrative an extraordinary consolation. It spoke to me of finding the hand of God not only in the goodness of what is made, but in loss, disorientation, separation and the gift of new beginnings.

I first became aware of the healing power of the text in the context of the Easter liturgy. I had been asked to read it as the first lesson at the Paschal Vigil. It was about four o'clock in the morning. The church was quite dark. The congregation were in ones or twos scattered among the pews, huddled in overcoats against the cold. None of us was used to being in church at such a strange and awesome time of night. I read by the light of a tiny torch.

Time passes slowly just before dawn. The body's rhythm is not fully adjusted to consciousness. The long record of God's acts as Creator, with its solemn and repetitive pattern of separations and beginnings, moved and awed me as I read. It was almost like hearing an echo of the creation itself. These strange old human words seemed to carry a charge of something even stranger and more ancient, something that was becoming new and alive even as we listened. Just as the quasars in space carry a radio echo of the original explosion at the beginning of our universe, so the words of Genesis seemed to vibrate with the power of God's original meaning. Spoken to the scattered congregation they seemed to be a call to us to become God's people. Read by my eyes, processed by my brain and spoken through my mouth they seemed to be an invocation of God's word in the depths of my own being.

I came to recognise that the creation account in Genesis contains an alternating pattern of light and darkness, creation and separation. While it presents itself as an evocation of the creation of our universe, it also reminds us of the human processes of birth and growth and the development of consciousness that goes with those processes. We are all miniature universes in so far as we are creatures who insist on making meanings. So, whatever else it is about, the Genesis text is about the creation of *us*.

When I have discussed this thought with others they have sometimes been rather surprised, as though I was saying something new and original. But in fact the insight is a very old one, and goes back even before the Christian era. The ancient text of Genesis has hardly ever been read as though it were a detached and clinical report of how God made the universe. It has always been seen for what it is, a *religious* text, a text about meanings and origins, rather than a description of processes. This should not surprise us. Over and over again the scriptures interpret themselves in mystical terms. Scripture is also, and endlessly, commentary on other parts of scripture. No single meaning can be taken as God-given or permanent. There are layers of meaning which need to be negotiated. The literal, the symbolic, the personal, the prophetic all have their place. The Church knows this, and yet sometimes resists knowing that it knows. The Church exploits the fluidity of scripture when there is a need for doctrinal development and re-interpretation, and yet it hides this process from itself because it also wants to affirm the unity and continuity of revealed truth.

As individual believers we need access both to the many-layered pattern of the scriptures, and the security of belonging within a tradition, to which we may contribute by faithful and honest criticism. It is easier for lay people to do this than for clergy, and easier for Anglicans than for Catholics or conservative evangelicals Nevertheless the task belongs to all of us. All are called to pray with integrity of mind and heart.

Praying with scripture
If this is true then it affects the way we read the Bible. It makes it possible for us to see our own story in it, and it makes it possible for us to allow biblical texts to carry different meanings at different times. We are so hammered over the heads by

fundamentalists who insist that they are the only people who treat the scriptures seriously. I think they misunderstand the nature of scripture in a way that is spiritually damaging. We are also, I think, subtly undermined by the assumptions of liberal scholarship, which limits meaning to what can be deduced through the rigours of historical enquiry. Common to fundamentalists and liberals is a woodenness and deadness about understanding the Bible. The text cannot breathe because it is strangled in the assumptions of one or the other school of thought.

To integrate our theology and our spirituality I think we need to be aware of three ways of looking at scripture. First we need to know, as far as we can, what the text meant to those who originally composed it. Second, we need to think out what it can mean now, in the light of our knowledge and common experience. And third, I need to discern what it means to me and to the relationships which are forming me.

Biblical scholarship can help us with the first part. There are plenty of useful commentaries on Genesis. I have not spent much time on this aspect except where it very directly affects the way we might pray with the text. The second part is harder. I am aware that there are scientists who believe that we shall soon have a unified and total description of the universe in physical terms. I am not prepared to defend Genesis as a rival theory, because I believe this is to misunderstand the nature of its inspiration. But neither do I want to limit the interpretation of the text to inner spiritual processes. I am always excited by hints that the discoveries of physics and biology might, in some way, mirror the processes of emotional and spiritual development that we recognise in human experience. I am aware that the attempt to crystallise these hints into theories is to move on to dangerous ground, but I believe that to ignore the hints is intellectual and spiritual folly. After all, our universe is one, and we carry in every cell of our body the material elements that were created in the first microseconds of the big bang. We *are* made of the same stuff as the stars.

But in the end I can only appropriate this text if I am prepared to engage with the third way of knowing. I need to get to grips with it in personal terms.

I have been very much helped by discovering the use of the

imagination in prayer and relating the insights of scripture study to my own and others' experience. For many years I lived and worked in an agnostic world as a television producer and film-maker. I am now ordained and help to train men and women for the priesthood. When I worked in television it was important to me not to insulate my faith from the effects of that pressured, exciting and sometimes terrifying environment. Now that I work for the Church it is important me not to lose touch with my 'secular' self. I am a person who needs thinking time, space, silence and company. I also need the discipline of regular times of prayer. Without prayer I dry up at the roots. Faith, intuition, the discoveries of science and the arts of psychology persuade me that it is possible that the universe makes sense. I have come to believe that inner experience and outer reality do mirror each other, even though this mirroring cannot be wholly described. The mystical and the sensible need each other if we are to come to truth. So the prayer that I am working towards is both personal and universal, rational and emotional, detached and intimate. To pray with Genesis means that we cannot afford to leave anything out. In the long run it is the whole of created reality that we meet in this text: time, space, history, the unconscious, the future of the planet and the cosmos, sex, love, sleep, birth and death.

Day One

The Eyes of Light

In the beginning when God created the heavens and the earth, the earth was a formless void, and darkness covered the face of the deep while the Spirit of God swept over the face of the waters.

Then God said, 'Let there be light'; and there was light. And God saw that the light was good; and God separated the light from the darkness. God called the light Day, and the darkness he called Night. And there was evening and there was morning, the first day. (Gen. 1:1–5)

The word *genesis* means origin or beginning. The account of creation that we shall be trying to pray with is an attempt to penetrate the mystery of beginnings. It has to do with the universe and it has to do with us.

'Let there be light'

God creates the heavens and the earth by calling into existence *light*. God's first word is a word of permission. God gives the universe permission to be, and light is, significantly, the first thing other than God to exist. Why light? The early Christian fathers knew that this text was hinting at more than the creation of physical light. Light, to them, was a profound metaphor for consciousness. The universe is not only called into being by God. It is given, at its genesis, in its origin, the possibility of becoming conscious of itself. It has the potential for becoming a vast communications system. This is what we see happening, and we see it more clearly than the priests of Israel who composed our text. Through the techniques of advanced astronomy we human beings are able to receive signals that come to us from the first few seconds of the

6

universe's existence. The galaxies and stars *talk* to themselves of their past creations and catastrophes. They talk in waves of light and sound and radiation. But only beings with the gift of consciousness can interpret the signals into knowledge.

Whenever I read those first words I have a mental picture of God as a great brooding shadow, surrounding a hollow space out of which stars and suns and whole galaxies are flowing in a dark and unearthly silence. It is beautiful and rather terrifying. That picture tells you more about me than about God, yet without such pictures I cannot begin to know what God means to me. I cannot begin to pray in truth. It is better to admit the pictures, even if they mislead. If I do not I may be dominated by other, unconscious, and even more misleading ones.

Between the given text and the mental image is the possibility of change. Between the words of Genesis and my picture is the possibility of prayer. The text is written by human beings, and I read it as myself, a particular person. Yet it also comes to me as a divine word, as the word of God, and it tells me that God is creating.

God is creating worlds, God is creating me. I am unfinished and so is the world. I can place myself within 'the heavens and the earth' of God's activity and know that God is not static, God creates change, and the God who creates change in the stars is the God who changes me.

Through aeons of cosmological and biological evolution this possibility of prayer is created afresh in each human being. God's word of permission, 'Let there be light', is a personal word addressed to each one of us. Each one of us has the chance to recognise ourselves as God's unique and beloved creatures. We are creatures with eyes who can see and be seen.

In those first words of Genesis there is such a balance of power and restraint. God's word is both an explosion and a holding back, a rush of divine energy and a sacrifice of divine omnipotence. The universe is given permission to be: 'Let there be light.' Being and consciousness flood out from the word of God. Stars are the eyes of light and so are minds and angels.

How can I pray with this text? How can I make it part of the process of becoming that only I can do?

God is God. His first word to you, to me, is a word of

permission. God does not want to be the whole universe. God does not want to be you or me. God wants to be God. God brings you into being, just as he brings the rest of the universe into being as something other than himself.

God creates the possibility of consciousness that will flood the universe with sound and light and song and meaning. In just the same way, and as part of the same process, each one of us is created as a unique, personal point of consciousness. You are one unrepeatable interface between conscious and unconscious reality. You are the creation of the word and Spirit of God. God has never made you before and will never make you again.

God's gift of freedom

God makes you for freedom which only you can enjoy. Your personal freedom is part of the wider freedom of the whole universe. God has created the whole cosmos to be 'liberated from its bondage to decay' (Rom. 8:21). The destiny of the universe is not chaos but glory. In the same way each one of us is created for freedom. We are to become ourselves, to be whole and fulfilled, and this is God's gift to us. God's gifts need to be received and enjoyed. God's gifts to human beings can only be received and enjoyed by human beings, by *persons*. Persons are not quite the same as solitary individuals, nor are they a crowd. Persons are living networks of biology and emotions and memories and relationships. Each is unique, but none can flourish alone. Each in some way contains others, and is contained by others, without his or her personal truth ever being wholly isolated or exhausted. Persons are beings who live by exchange. We live from exchanges of power and strength, exchanges of milk and blood, sweat and semen; exchanges of sympathy and support, exchanges of ideas and insights. Within these exchanges, to be human means to know love and hate, intimacy and aloneness.

God's gift, to be the person who you are, a person with gifts to share and hopes to be fulfilled, needs to be received and enjoyed by you. Otherwise the gift remains homeless and detached, roaming the earth. God invites you to freedom: 'Let there be light.' God invites you to being and consciousness.

Reactions to such an invitation will differ. Perhaps you hear the invitation as a chance to be *de*-lighted. You can relax and enjoy God's word to you with a sense of trust and spontaneous thankfulness. Perhaps you hear it as relief. Freedom to be yourself at last! Or perhaps you hear it as demand. The very word 'freedom' may ring in your mind as a word of threat, foreshadowing failure, or as one more thing to feel guilty about.

Christians in general feel guilty about many things. As you will know, the causes of guilt are endless. There is no need to add to them. You know that you do not pray enough. I have a growing pile of books on various aspects of spirituality, most of which I will probably never read. And here I am, making one more! There are also periods in my life when I experience a profound reluctance to pray, a nagging sense of dislocation and anxiety with known forms of prayer. Praying is not the only thing to feel guilty about, however. You probably also know that you do not play enough either. You should relax more. Jog regularly or play squash. Make more time for your families and friends, for real leisure, for flopping in front of the telly. Perhaps you secretly fear that you do not work hard enough, that you are really unspeakably lazy and selfish, and that if you don't push yourself, someone might notice.

All this you know. If you are an average anxious twenty-first century Christian, you will almost certainly be a bit of a Pelagian, perhaps a closet perfectionist, subject to guilt and stress. Your life probably feels fraught with pressures, some of which you know are accidental, some of which are inevitable, and at least some of which you know you have brought on yourself by living in permanent overdrive. Clergy suffer peculiarly acutely from these pressures, but lay people are also not immune. Many kill themselves with church work and church commitments.

I remember meeting a famous British evangelist who told me, as if it would be the crowning achievement of grace in his life, that he did not expect to be around to draw his old age pension. He considered it a virtue to burn his life out for the gospel, and no doubt drew his family into making the sacrifices which made his sacrifice possible.

Yet life is precious and it is God's gift. Most of us might prefer to find a balance of work and play and prayer which will enable us to live rather than to die. It is not all that clear from the tradition (and certainly not from the book of Genesis) that God requires us to make bloody and mangled sacrifices of ourselves and our families in his service.

Getting the balance right is difficult though. In my former life as a television producer, and now as a priest I find I am far from immune from nagging guilt and a sense of failure. I know I am most attentive and most creative when I allow myself time to relax and play, but the pressures of the job have always made that difficult. Working in television, it was the fear of failure and the competitiveness of the environment which worked up stress and anxiety; in the Church it is a sense that the job is never done, however many hours you put in. Like many people I seem to need a certain amount of guilt and stress to drive myself to make decisions. When I worked in television the results of my efforts were visible on the screen and publicly open to judgement. This induced fear as well as guilt. Images from my films seeped into my dreams and got muddled up with the people that I knew in everyday life. Now I work in the Church I dream of long, vague processions moving endlessly through churches and cathedrals, never finding their destination, or of losing my sermon notes, or of struggling into my cassock and finding it is torn or too tight. Some of the dreams I used to have in my earlier life are still with me, especially those which suggest panic! I frequently dream of aeroplanes crashing and cars running out of control. I am drawn to the writings of Christian mystics and to the disciplines of contemplative prayer, but I sometimes think it is because the very *thought* of contemplating God comes as such a contrast to the rest of my life that it gives me a sense of relief. My own actual attempts at contemplation are far less impressive than the books I read before flopping asleep.

I remember one evening shortly before I was to conduct a retreat. I was sitting in a dark recording area at Television Centre in London supposedly supervising the transfer of a film to videotape for transmission the following week. Everything went wrong. The computer, which contained stacks of pre-timed and pre-coded subtitles within its memory, presented them at the wrong moment. The credits refused to be visible. The beautiful new film print, which represented six months' work, was becoming visibly ragged and dirty. In the middle of this my film editor (a somewhat abrasive evangelical Christian

who read theological books while eating his lunchtime sand-
wiches) leaned over to me as I sat wriggling with visible
unhappiness and anxiety and said, 'You're not very good at
contemplation in the midst of action, are you?' We know that
we do not pray or play enough, and it is possible that the
invitation to receive God's gift of being and consciousness
might be heard as one more demand, one more thing we have
to do, or succeed in, 'one more bloody thing' to add to all the
rest.

God is God. Some traditions of Christian spirituality have
imaged God as a being who wanted to become everything, a
God engaged in a ruthless take-over bid for the universe of his
creation. Yet the Bible seems to prefer to think of God as if
God has real boundaries. There is God, and there is not God,
and the good news is that God desires to be God for us. God
wants to be our God, the God who is making us, the God of
grace. He wants to be known as the one who takes the
pressure off, who lifts the burden of our anxiety and guilt.

The prophet Hosea speaks of God bending down to his
over-burdened creature and loosening the yoke on its jaws,
soothing its stress (Hos. 11:4). Again and again the prophets of
the Bible remind God's people of their history. The God of
the Bible is a liberating God, a God committed in love to
everyone who is oppressed, burdened or weak. Again and
again God's people are reminded to look at their past and
discern God as the one who takes the pressure off. In the same
way God wants to be with us as we reflect on our own personal history.

Ash Wednesday

I remember a particular Ash Wednesday when I was staying
with a friend in Birmingham. The air was thick with snow
turning to sleet. We walked through the cold along slippery
pavements towards the chapel of the College of the Ascension.
It was just before seven. We were going to a Eucharist to mark
the beginning of Lent. I remember feeling as cold and grey as
the sky outside, and also tired in body and mind. The cele-
brant invited us to be present to the meaning of the liturgy in
the words: 'Remember O man that thou art dust'. Then he
marked our foreheads with ashes.

In this simple gesture each member of the little early morning congregation was being reminded that we human beings belong to both life and death. We are creatures of earth and time, linked to all other life forms in our capacities for birth, growth, sex and death. There is no escape from this fundamental truth of our existence. Whatever we know of our own individuality, whatever we believe about God is boun-daried by this knowledge: 'Remember that thou art dust'.

If we want to learn to pray and to grow in the knowledge of God, then this is where we start from. We start with dust, with earth, with *humus* as human beings, evolved from earth as earth spins in space. The challenge is to remember yourself as the changing creature of a God who creates change.

God wants to reconnect with you in your uniqueness, with the you that is the role you play in life, and with the you who is more than that role. God seeks out the lost sheep, the lost coin. God looks in the dark as well as the light. God seeks out the lost and hidden bits of us which are necessary for our completion. God is God and comes to us where we are, not where we feel we ought to be. The God of grace is always a God of beginnings. If you have set aside time to know yourself as God's, maybe the first thing you will discover about yourself is that you are very, very tired. Simply admitting this is a kind of freedom. It is freedom to admit that you are not omnipo-tent. It is freedom to admit that you are not as competent as you would like to be at managing your time and your physical and emotional resources. It is freedom to be able to admit that your mind is jangled, or that the mechanisms of feeling and thinking are overstrained. The night after my evening of technical disasters I felt like a machine whose circuits were overloaded, on the point of fusing, burning-out.

The pressures that prevent freedom

A sense of almost unbearable strain, of pressure, is common among those who minister and care in God's Church and in God's world. Bishops and clergy and caring Christians are simply battered by the pressures on their lives and on their time. We try to encourage people to persevere in their faith, to attend Church and to take on responsibility for the Church's life. But so often we are simply inviting them to spend even more of their energies keeping the Church going, at expense to their own well-being. Some of them collude with these pressures, because relentless activity helps to quench our guilt and provide us with a sense of worth. So we contribute to the problem out of our own unresolved need for healing and re-creation. On the other hand some church members are beginning to simply refuse to play this game and will not take on any responsibilities at all. Commitments to the Church are commitments too many.

The problem of over-activity is wider and deeper than our personal stories. We are afflicted by the pressure to justify ourselves, a pressure which is entwined, like a great and spreading plant, in the soil of our society. The plant must produce, and produce it does. Deeds, results, productivity, good works. It is a plant bearing good and evil in different seasons and in different persons, and we must learn to recognise its different fruits and distinguish their effects on us. Some are healthy, some are deadliest poison. The need to justify ourselves affects believers and those who minister to believers as a particular form of anxiety which arises because we are not very sure of the place of religion in our society. Sometimes it seems religion has a place. In our individual lives, at death and at birth perhaps, and at marriage, for those who want their nuptials blessed. In national life religion appears in times of crisis and disaster, as a unifying force and a container for emotions that would be too big to express in any other way. Religion hangs on, it seems, in extreme situations. This is disturbing for those who are seeking God in their daily lives, and hope to find him, not only in the extremes of experience but in the familiar, routine, lovely and boring bits. I once heard a television critic describe religion as a 'minor branch of psychology', and I think he meant that for some rather peculiar people religion was a kind of therapeutic game which had the same kind of beneficial effects as football watching or fishing or encounter groups.

As religious people we are often uneasy with the word 'religion'. We are not very sure, with the whole of ourselves, what we are doing or why or for whom. This uncertainty leads to a long lack of confidence and internal dividedness. There is an aggressive and growing hostility in wider society towards people of faith. Some find the whole idea of a creator

God a kind of personal insult which they want to see extir-
pated from public consciousness, or at least relegated to the
private life of the individual. As individuals we do not know
what is expected of us by God's word of permission to be. It
might mean putting our heads above the parapet in a hostile
world. Still less do we know what demands freedom might
make on us. At least, we could probably cope with a list of
demands. More demands are things we dutiful Christian people
have become rather good at. What is harder is the thing itself,
freedom, the voice that says tantalisingly, without explanation
or instruction, 'Be'. Yet even in our uncertainty we are in a
privileged position to discover what freedom means.

I realised this in a particularly sharp way on a visit to what is
now the borderlands of Bosnia-Herzegovina and Croatia in
the former Yugoslavia. At the time I was working on a film[1]
for the Everyman series about a remarkable series of apparitions of the Virgin Mary to a group of young people in the
village of Medjugorje. Catholics in the region comprised a
strong and clearly identified minority. They were not greatly
loved by the rest of the population. Freedom of worship was
guaranteed by the constitution but, as in most socialist states,
the price of public confession of faith was considerable for
most people. Being an active believer required moral strength
and dedication. The apparitions certainly contributed to a
sense of renewal among many of the priests and nuns who
ministered to the Catholic community. I found these men and
women to be impressive human beings. There was a vigour
and a vitality about them, a sense of purpose, humour and
energy which contrasted with the worried Christianity of the
supposedly free West. These men and women knew what they
were doing. They knew what their God-given tasks were.
However hard and costly life was for them (and it could be
very costly, dangerous and lonely) they were acting out of
their strengths. They were not afraid to show anger when they
found their phones had been tapped or cut off. They were not
afraid to show passion about the gospel. They were not afraid
to denounce what they considered to be evil.

There are western Christians today who would envy such

---

[1] *The Madonna of Medjugorje*, BBC/Westernhanger.

strength and see it as freedom, and even try to act as if they lived under similar oppressions. A former member of the Archbishops' Council of the Church of England suggested, when she left that body, that serious persecution lay ahead for those who followed Christ in Britain. It was an extreme statement, and was backed by little evidence. I almost felt, on reading it, that it was what she wished to see happen; to make Christianity more vigorous and interesting. But there is as yet no sign of this persecution coming about, merely indifference, shading into mild hostility. Maybe the strange freedom that a genuinely persecuted Church might enjoy is not the freedom that is given to us. Our spiritual struggle, our context for finding freedom is different. We live in a greyer and more twilight world. Here the distinctions between belief and unbelief are not so clear-cut. We have to cope with ambivalence. We have to get to know the unbeliever who lives inside our own hearts. We also have to learn to recognise the true believer who stands outside all religious structures. We have to discover the glory and the desolation of the Lord in television and suburbia, in the city and in the dole queue, in the visible churches and in the invisible communities which are always coming to be as signs of God among us. All this is draining and tiring and difficult and undermining. We cannot blame our spiritual problems on a godless government or on spying or persecuting neighbours.

So the reasons why Christian people experience tiredness, confusion and burnout are genuine. They are forms of persecution from within, and it is our part of God's purpose to struggle with them. In the middle of our struggle God calls us into our freedom.

Here, God says, you can lay down the burden for a time. Here, in the attempt to pray, in the attempt to re-member yourself as God's creature, is a new beginning. 'Let there be light.' Being, consciousness. You. Me. God is God. And God wants to be God for you and for me. He wants you to know yourself as his beloved. His chosen one. And it is not so easy because much of us is programmed for guilt and death.

Even the Croatian Christians did not find praying easy. Mild, or even intense disapproval does not necessarily make it easier to find God for oneself, though the sense of group solidarity might be greater.

In fact the invitation to be is never wholly welcome because we are never wholly formed. To be more fully, and to become more conscious requires a consent to growth and change which may frighten and exhaust us, particularly when we are tired or depressed.

The inner wasteland

When I set aside a period of time for prayer, or when I go on retreat, I am often aware of a feeling of dread and darkness that hovers around me, mingled with the genuine and urgent desire to slow down and enjoy the opportunity to be with God. I used to think that this dread arose from the fact that I was concealing some appalling sin, or even an emotional sickness of which I was unaware, and which might paralyse me with anxiety once I was alone with it. It now seems to me that this sense of darkness is very natural and very obvious. Times of prayer and being alone open us up, not only to the light of consciousness but to the dark of what is unformed and unknown in our own personalities. There are some who believe that people are afraid of contemplation because the stillness of it reminds them of the stillness we associate with death. Certainly we feel fragile, because at certain levels we are fragile. We come to be persons out of a watery chaos of possibilities. The text of Genesis insists that God's word is spoken over a sea of darkness, 'waste and void', as the King James Bible puts it. Yet this is creative ground. The Spirit of God hovers over the confusion. God breathes upon it and speaks into it, and no wonder the darkness is ruffled and stirred. Augustine described this anxiety as he meditated on the creation of the universe in his *Confessions* (Book XI.9):

Who can understand this mystery or explain it to others? What is that light whose gentle beams now and again strike through to my heart, causing me to shudder in awe yet firing me with their warmth? I shudder to feel how different I am from it: yet in so far as I am like it, I am aglow with its fire.

Augustine cannot bear the glow of recognition for very long: 'But when I weakly fall away from its light, those clouds envelop me again in the dense mantle of darkness which I bear for my punishment. For "my strength ebbs away for very misery" so that I cannot sustain my blessings.'

This is the problem. Augustine does have some sense of being greeted, known and blessed by God. But he cannot quite relax into that knowledge. He is insecure, confused by God's greeting, not knowing what it might mean. Perhaps he is happier falling into the dense mantle of darkness in which he can know himself, simply, as a wretched sinner.

Or, perhaps you would rather work yourself to the bone being useful, doing things for other people, than allow yourself to be greeted by God. Or perhaps you want to put off that greeting until you feel in better shape inside yourself, until you have organised the internal economy of your life and are *ready* to be found by God. Or perhaps your self-image is so calm, so unmarked by anxiety or sadness that you cannot imagine what all the fuss is about. Human beings have devised extra-ordinarily persuasive and intricate ways of avoiding God. Nobody who is found by God in the Bible ever seems to have been ready for the encounter. God is always a God of wonder, surprise, miracle; one who appears in flaming bushes and desert wastes, and even, unexpectedly, in the middle of a formal liturgy where everything seemed to be well under control; God is one who interrupts our journey as angels, wayfarers and strangers.

So whatever is going to happen as you begin to pray with this text, it is going to be a mixture of light and darkness, an invitation to freedom and a sense of *un*-freedom. This is what the scriptures teach us and what the tradition affirms. Yet your experience of darkness and light, freedom and un-freedom, will be uniquely yours, as original to you as your fingerprints.

'God saw that the light was good.' When God sees you coming into being, as the self that you are, there is rejoicing in heaven. The light simply delights God. I like to think of it making him laugh. It delights God whether it is the light that leaps between galaxies, or the light of a laser that cuts steel and burns out disease, or the light of human consciousness growing towards wisdom and worship. Light is light, and it is part of the physical world. It is also sign and symbol of the one who creates the universe and us.

But then there is the dark. God does not reject the dark ground of creation. The formless waste – the place that reminds us of sleep and death, rest and monsters, anxiety, depression and possibility – is the place where God's Spirit broods. The Spirit dreams new life out of the dark waters, unimagined forms out of emptiness and formlessness.

'There was evening and there was morning, one day'

God's acts of creation proceed in ordered rhythm. We shall see that there is separation, naming and darkness. Then there is new light, new creation, separation, naming and darkness again.

With the dawn of the possibility of consciousness has come a kind of time. Not time as we think of it. Time as we think of it is historical time, a way of measuring out what happens, as one thing after another. That sort of time must wait for the creation of the sun and moon and stars. But this is time as rhythm, regularity, repetition, order. It is time that assures us that God's universe has predictability. God's universe is not chaos, but cosmos. A framework of being and meaning is coming into focus and rhythm is part of its structure. Dark and light are separated out and given definition. Morning and evening are one day. What is the place of the dark in this? Dark is named as night, yet dark would not be known as dark without light. It would simply be formlessness. There is a problem here. For darkness can either be seen as part of the totality of God's creation, the shadow made by the creation of light; or it can be seen as what God repudiates and triumphs over in his first command. This ambivalence has never been satisfactorily solved in the whole history of Christian theology and spirituality. So don't expect it to be solved here!

Two languages

What we can do though, is to recognise that two theological languages are meeting in the Genesis passage. We can make ourselves aware of the unresolved clash between them. One language is that of revelation and divine creation. God creates from nothing. He is free. There is no pre-existent something out of which he forms the universe. This is the great insight of monotheism: 'In the beginning, God...' It is this freedom of God which guarantees our freedom. We are created by one who allows us creativity. God does not want to be everything. God wants to be God. He is not envious of the powers he has given us. He wants us to be free.

Yet 'the earth was without form and void, and darkness was upon the face of the deep'. Here, it seems, is another language, describing a dark watery something which precedes God's specific acts of creation. The church fathers, reflecting on this passage, tried to insist that the formless, empty earth either meant nothing at all, or that it was created by God before creation, perhaps before time itself.[2]

Their attempts are not wholly convincing. For this second language carries echoes of an ancient mythology which is present in other parts of the Bible, and has important resonances for us as we try to understand the scriptures. Bible scholars know that this passage in Genesis was the creation of priestly writers, theologians, who were trying to articulate the faith of Israel in a coherent, durable form. They were working, probably in Babylon, in exile from Israel, five hundred years before the birth of Jesus. All over the ancient Near East there were accounts of the creation seen in terms of battles between gods; the most famous, and the one which may have been known to the authors of the Genesis passage, comes from ancient Babylonia. Marduk the creator god slays Tiamat the chaos monster, and out of her pierced body the worlds are formed. The creator god in this mythology is not free. He creates out of struggle with other aspects of divinity. In such a mythology the world rests on divine ambivalence, and it is the terrifying fate of human beings to have to endure that ambivalence without any hope of resolving it. The priests of Israel composed their account to affirm the oneness of God and his freedom in creation. But as they struggled for words that were 'clean' of mythological overtones they found themselves at the limits of language. Echoes of the old cosmic battle still exist in the text, and are much more obvious to us than they would have been to them. The language of 'waste and void' is the nearest they could get to 'nothing', but it still doesn't quite feel like nothing! Even though they were composing a hymn of God's freedom which is also a foundation document for our struggles for human freedom, they reflected something of the old language of divine ambivalence and human bondage.

[2] See, for example, Augustine's rather tortuous argument in *Confessions*, Book XII.

When we pray with the creation account and try to read our own creation in it, we need to remember that there are two languages here, the old language of myth and the new language of revelation. The dark ground described by the myth language is not divine, and it is not quite the same as nothing.[3] I cannot resolve the ontological problem of the 'waste and void', but I can at least find a place in human experience which could correspond to it.

In fact what it reminds us of, in a rather remarkable way, is what we know about our own beginnings in time. We can read it as a description of our own coming into existence. We can hear it telling us that we came from the womb and from unconsciousness, and that before that, we were nothing. It reminds us that what we are being formed out of here and now, as we continue to develop, is something unknown to us, something nevertheless which God's Spirit moves over and breathes upon, something which has the potential for a richer, deeper life than we could ever envisage with only our conscious minds and desires.

So we can take courage in the experience of prayer. The God we seek is reliable to his promise and to his nature, he is a free God who longs for our freedom. The word 'let there be light' comes to us as gospel. The dark truth that is also part of us is not rejected. It is where the Spirit of God hovers, troubling our memory with discoveries yet to be made.

Summary

'Let there be light' is God's first word. It brings into existence our universe and gives it the possibility of producing consciousness. Because each one of us is a point of consciousness, a universe in miniature, we can also hear 'let there be light' as a personal word calling us to become more conscious of our true selves and God. This is an invitation to freedom.

Our reactions to God's invitation will differ. We look at some of the personal, social and ecclesiastical pressures which

[3] This is not the place to embark on a philosophical digression on the doctrine of *creatio ex nihilo*. I do believe, nevertheless, that some modern theology too easily equates the Genesis account with the developed doctrine, and thus limits the hermeneutical possibilities of this text.

block our attempts to become free. We then reflect on the disturbance that God's call provokes in us. Consciousness makes us aware of unconsciousness, light reminds us of dark. The composition of the Genesis text reflects two opposing strands. The dominant note is the priestly theology of God's freedom and creativity. But there are undertones of a darker, pagan mythology.

Praying with the text requires us to be aware of both aspects. For our human journey is from the unconsciousness of the womb life, to conscious maturity in God. We need to hold on to both aspects, not rejecting the dark but recognising and differentiating the darkness and the light as we meet them in our experience.

Suggestions for prayer

1 Read the passage from Genesis slowly to yourself. Try repeating the phrase 'Let there be light'. Notice your feelings and thoughts.
2 Light a candle. Sit quite still and watch it carefully. Again, as far as you can without self-judgement, notice your feelings and thoughts.
3 Read Psalm 139 slowly to yourself. Find any bits in it which you want to say to God. Then say them, aloud or in your heart.
4 Find any old photographs of yourself as a child, or pictures that were taken at significant moments of your life. Share them, if you can, with God. If you cannot, notice why and tell God about it.
5 Try to remember a time when you have experienced a sense of your own freedom, or when you have been released from a burden. What was the result? Share any feelings or thoughts with God.
6 Is there any area of your life which feels cramped, hurt, dead or hemmed in? Can you name it, and identify it in God's presence? If you laugh bitterly because all your life feels like that, share that with God too.
7 Read the passage from Genesis again. Then repeat your own name to yourself, either aloud or in your heart. Try to hear God calling you into existence, by name.

Day Two

The World's Womb

And God said, 'Let there be a dome in the midst of the waters, and let it separate the waters from the waters.' And God made the dome and separated the waters that were under the dome from the waters that were above the dome. And it was so. God called the Dome Sky. And there was evening and there was morning, the second day. (Gen. 1:6–8)

The writers of Genesis imagined the unmade universe as a vast undifferentiated sea. God's creative light shines, and immediately there is separation and primeval order. Light is contrasted with dark, day with night. Everything is still liquid mush.

A space-time universe

God now hollows a space out of the waters. To hold the space open he constructs a huge dome, the first solid thing, the curve of the heavens as it looks to human eyes. This is what we see above us as the sky. The space in which we live, this environment, is held open for us, and boundaried, by the will of God. So this part of the Genesis passage has to do with the space-time environment in which we find ourselves. I believe that the authors knew that their writings would be understood on a number of different levels. They were not cosmologists but priests. Their purpose was to point out the hand of God in the wonder of their surroundings. In trying to do so they present a surprisingly convincing model of the conditions of our existence.

On a simple literal level the writers of Genesis could look up at the sky and see the blue dome of heaven. The blueness reminded them of what they assumed was wild sea above and beyond, held back by the great clear dome of the sky. We too, even with our more sophisticated science, can be moved to awe by the space-time environment in which we find ourselves. It is remarkable that this small planet, at the back end of an insignificant galaxy, should be a womb of life and consciousness. Faith can see the desire of God in clearing the way for our world out of the universe's sea of possibilities. Our earth atmosphere cradles us from the sky, and the as yet uninhabitable universe beyond. The dome of heaven is still the boundary which protects us and guarantees the space in which we live. Perhaps the time is coming when we shall be born into the wider universe through space exploration. That will involve us in a different sort of relationship with the earth, our first home. The astronauts and moon voyagers of recent times have helped us to appreciate the truth of our dependence on earth in a wholly new way. From the moon the earth is beautiful, and extraordinary. Green, blue, clouded and full of life and mystery. It is a living planet. From the standpoint of faith the capacity to bear life is what God gives to our bit of the universe on the second day of creation.

Discovering our own space and boundaries

These are ideas we can pray with and reflect on. But we also need to go further, to go down a layer, as it were, and make sense of the scripture in human terms. This passage speaks to us of the preciousness and the precariousness of human existence. Our life is held in balance between the deep blue sea above and the deep blue sea below. Above and below, what surrounds us cannot be wholly assimilated by our conscious processes. We come to consciousness from the unconsciousness of the womb life, and we pass into the dissolution of death, often through a final coma. It is in between, in space and time, personally lived through, that we are given permission to be and to become.

Out of watery nothingness God makes space for us. He creates the conditions necessary for conscious life. He creates the personal conditions necessary for your life and mine. The challenge to us, as we pray with this passage, is to discern his work in the space and boundaries of our personal lives. We can do this in the confidence that our growth into selfhood is part of the same process that is energising the whole universe. It is a holy quest, a path of life, a pilgrimage.

It has been fashionable for some years to use spatial metaphors to describe our condition and attitudes. We talk about 'where we are coming from', and even 'where we are *at*'. We understand these expressions as having something to do with our personal history. We might tell someone something about a past experience so that they can understand 'how I got to *where I am* today'.

Busy and anxious people, aware of the stress in their lives, also talk about the need for 'personal space'. A demand for more space has become a way of negotiating a change in a relationship, often a termination. 'I need space' has become a polite way of saying 'Leave me alone'. But if we need space, we also need boundaries. Busy and anxious people are often terrified of aloneness, of the un-boundaried, desert landscape of illness, failure or unemployment. Such catastrophes fill the mind and heart with dread that often takes the form of images reminiscent of the 'waste and void' before the first day of creation. What is feared is precisely a return to the pre-creation state, a place without order that reminds us of the dissolution of death. Work, routine, domesticity and duty are boundaries which force us to act, to do, to know ourselves as energetic and life-giving.

Without space we are in danger of being invaded and destroyed by our environment, deprived of our being. Without boundaries we are re-merged to our environment, unable to act, deprived of all vitality.

So a meditation on this passage becomes an attempt to become aware of the emotional and spiritual geography of our existence. This existence is not only set in boundaried space, as it were, but in a rhythm which, again, we may begin to discern. Pattern, cycle, repetition. The things which happen in our lives may appear random, but between the events and their outcome our own patterns of interpretation emerge, which enable us to make what happens to us make sense as part of our story.

It is in my own boundaried space, within my own rhythm, that God finds me and makes me, and I hear the word of God.

The first time this struck me was by accident. I am not

particularly gifted or organised at painting and decorating. I was setting up some bookshelves and I realised that they needed varnishing. To reach the top ones I had to stand on a chair and stretch, the tin of varnish in one hand and the paintbrush in another. The radio was on. I had been enjoying the varied menu of a Radio 4 morning when, to my annoyance, the wavelengths split. I was tuned to VHF and found myself with schools programmes. I was too precariously positioned to get down and retune, so I switched off mentally and concentrated on what I was doing. In the background the programme went on. It was a music and movement programme for the under fives. It sounded very like the programmes I remembered listening to when I had been that age. I was half-amused, half-annoyed by the well-modulated confiding tone of the radio actors as they delivered their instructions to their young listeners with appropriate atmospheric music in the background: 'Now, it is a cold winter's day, and the wind is blowing in the bare trees. Now it begins to snow. You are a snowflake, falling out of the sky and coming to rest on the ground...' Appropriate snowflake music followed. 'So now, be a snowflake, twirling down to the ground...' I pictured groups of little children at playschools standing on tiptoes and wobbling round the floor in time with the cold, twinkly snowflake music. 'Now, stand still in your own space.' The music came to an end.

'Stand still in your own space'

I stood on my chair, half-way between the floor and the ceiling. I had no choice but to stand still. But I could picture the children at the end of their snowflake dance standing up in their space, perhaps not quite as still as the instruction required, but still aware of themselves and their bodies, and attentive. 'Stand still in your own space.' The words were so simple, and yet they seemed to contain a profound resonance. I found myself wanting to do more than stand still. I wanted to rest in the words, to take them into myself. I could not quite recognise why it was important for me. Nor could I forget it. I went on with my varnishing, and the programme continued, but I could not get the words out of my mind: 'Stand still in your own space.'

As I reflected on it I found I was hearing the words as
though they were words of God. I found myself remembering
the Lord's words to Moses at the burning bush: 'Take your
shoes off your feet, for the place on which you stand is holy
ground' (Exod. 3:5).

'Stand still in your own space' sounded like a challenge to
me to stand my ground before the living God, to know my
own space and boundaries as the environment in which the
living God would appear to me. I was struck by the word
'stand'. For often, I think, I crawl or crouch before God in fear
or false humility. Sometimes I stretch or fly with unreality and
inflated ideas. Yet to stand before God is to occupy space
realistically, to be seen and to see. I was also struck by the
instruction to stand 'in your own space'. For often the
temptation is to stand in someone else's.

I found myself thinking of how often men encourage
women to stand in their space, in their shadow, and then
complain that they feel suffocated. Women frequently believe
that they have no right to any space at all. They let it be carved
up by parents, husbands, employers, children. Then they
complain, but beneath the complaint is an unvoiced terror that
to stand might mean to stand alone, unloved and unwanted.
Standing in our own space is not so easy. Many years later I
heard this challenge addressed to me again. It was at the
beginning of a Russian Orthodox service of Vespers con-
ducted in the chapel of Westcott House. It was an ecumenical
occasion, only a minority of us were Orthodox. The priest, Fr
Raphael, invited us to participate in the liturgy in a way
unfamiliar to most of us busy, activist Christians. He asked us
to do nothing, but to 'stand before God', to simply be the
selves we were before the face of God. As the Russian mystic,
Theophan the Recluse put it in the nineteenth century, 'Put
your mind in your heart and stand before God all day long'.

Standing is one thing. But being still, really still is another.
For stillness implies contentedness, concentration, a sense of
being gathered together. Yet the way to stillness is haunted
with the fear of fixity, impotence, sterility and death. When
you are not used to it it can feel very uncomfortable.

Perhaps the way to learn how to stand still in our own space
is to learn it like toddlers do, through play and experiment.
Perhaps we need to learn to become as little children.

Holding and being

From psychology we know that the development of human personality is a long, enchanting and hazardous process. In the womb we exist in a boundaried, narrow space where there is no separation. All our needs are provided for. We have no sense of being an 'I'. The mother, however, does have a sense of her growing baby. She 'imagines' the baby as a whole developing, healthy human infant. Her body, and her desire 'hold' this baby, both in reality and in imagination. She does not just provide a womb. She is an emotional, physical and spiritual environment. Her desire for the baby and her concern for its life and well-being arise out of her desire for her husband, and so roots the baby in a set of already existing relationships. Yet she is the first and most important person in the life story of the new potential human being.

Years ago the child psychiatrist Donald Winnicott spoke to a radio audience of mothers about their role at the beginning of life:

> At the very beginning there is no difficulty because the baby is in you and part of you. Although only a lodger, so to speak, the baby in the womb joins up with all the ideas of babies you ever had, and at the beginning the baby actually is the secret. The secret becomes a baby ...[1]

The secret life, nurtured in physical reality and in imagination, becomes a real baby. The birth process with its mess and pain and hard work interrupts for ever the state of unconscious dreaming union between mother and child. Most babies survive this to find themselves in a bigger, colder, noisier world. Yet here, if all is well, they are greeted by good sensations, warmth, delight, protection. Their vulnerability is recognised. They are held. A new baby is not perceived as an uncoordinated collection of arms and legs and a floppy head. If all is well the baby is greeted as whole, totally in need of care, still belonging to its mother's body. In the first stages of a baby's life it is still unable to distinguish between itself and its mother-environment.

[1] 'More that Irks – and Why', script of BBC broadcast for series *Parents and Children*, 1960.

The nurturing security of the mother is everywhere and everything. At this stage the baby is in a position of total dependence. It is also in a position of tremendous 'power', as every exhausted mother knows. The baby's demands are unceasing. They intrude totally on her, overriding her own concerns and needs. Most mothers resent this at times, but they are bound up with the baby's vulnerability, and know that its needs must come first.

The baby is born with an innate capacity to develop physically and emotionally into a human person. What enables this development could be summed up simply as love. Human love is a creative environment, competent, warming, and protective. Human love *holds*, it is consistent. It is a love that welcomes the newborn one not only in his need, but in her individuality. This love is borne principally by the mother, but also by the father and other members of the family. It is never perfect, it is nearly always tinged with some elements of jealousy or resentment. But usually it is enough. If all is well the baby has a good chance of developing its unique personality. There is enough love and stability in the baby's universe to 'hold' it safe, and to enable healthy development.

If all is well, mothers and babies do enjoy quiet times of play and mutual enjoyment. Mouth to breast, eye to eye, small body enfolded by arm and lap. There is hunger, there is demand, there is food, there is excitement, there is satisfaction, there is quiet, there is a merging back into oneness. Our basic well-being depends on these fundamental experiences. Most of us have been loved enough to begin the process of growth into viable human beings.

As the process continues the baby begins to learn little patches of independence, separation. There is the development of real skills, of seeing and sensing and co-ordinating. Consciousness of self begins. This is sometimes bearable. It is sometimes agony. Some psychologists describe the meeting with reality as 'an insult'. The baby's sense of omnipotence is wounded by the knowledge of separation. Yet if there is enough predictability, if the separation is not too long, if the mother continues to hold and nurture and cherish and mirror back the baby to itself, then all will be well. A foundation of basic trust is laid. The baby's universe has a structure, the essence of which is a reliable rhythm of activity and rest, venture and safety. There is separation and naming, darkness and a new day, creation and satisfaction. And so we can begin to recognise a pattern for healthy human development. Security enables growth and development. Growth and development involve degrees of independence and separation.

Things that go wrong

Of course some things go wrong. No one comes through to maturity without some sort of damage. There are no perfect parents, no guarantees against illness, accident or congenital defect. There are plenty of opportunities for being scarred and hurt by the process that makes us. But if our environment is good enough we find ways of dealing with the damage. Many minor fractures and bruises can be healed by time, 'holding' and being understood.

Some hurts are not healed though. There are persons with tragically fractured personalities who limp through life in great pain and instability. Many more exist with buried wounds and angers that smoulder beneath the surface of consciousness, secretly dominating their lives and ruining relationships. There is damage everywhere, yet for most of us there is enough good experience to live on. One of the most creative of human arts is to find ways of incorporating our personal damage so that it contributes to our humanity rather than robbing us of it.

Here, each person's task is different. But in the end it is the process of how we got where we are that we need to understand if we are to become fully conscious human beings, reflecting the glory of the Lord. The ground that we stand on is holy ground, but we need to stand on it firmly with both feet.

Standing our ground

The ground we stand on is personal ground. It is the ground of our genetic inheritance, our family way of life, our emotional make-up and predispositions. Also our place in the family and the history of what has happened to us and what it has meant. From this ground the self grows, the self that is a mixture of strength and weakness, with its capacities for creativity and reflection, love and hate. It is this self that is invited to stand still in its own space and know itself as God's creation.

Of course earlier damage may have blocked our growth, or our desire to grow. If this has happened to you, you may find the invitation to stand still in your own space incomprehensible. Or it may suggest or remind of some deep and agonising pain. Or it may give rise to feelings of deadness, numbness and unreality. Many of us employ a false self for some of our transactions in the outer or inner world, or for our transactions with God. We cannot always help this. Sometimes it makes sense, in a dangerous world, not to reveal our true selves too easily. But sometimes the false self becomes stuck and inflexible. We mistake its hard defensiveness for the whole of us and complain of depression or an inability to feel. Or we find whenever anything goes wrong for us, we automatically cast the blame on to convenient others. Anything rather than feel the wound ourselves. We may indeed at times need a coat of armour against feeling, to protect us from some unassimilable horror or terror of childhood. But the armour can become a trap from which we find we cannot get out. Then we find we have locked ourselves in and thrown away the key.

Very often when people complain that they cannot pray, it is because they have lost any sense of being true and real in themselves. They have chosen instead to live their lives on the basis of the false self. Some do this by identifying with an idealised image of themselves. They act as if they were what they feel they should be, and not what they are. They have forgotten what they are and are genuinely puzzled by concepts of true and false selves. Prayer is difficult for such people because they are standing above their true space, detached from the passion and rage and excitement and tenderness of the body. They may think of themselves as being very special to God, but they find it hard to be intimate with God and to share their experience of crying, mourning and failure. Many charismatic Christian leaders suffer from these problems, and find it very difficult to share them honestly, because to do so would mean laying aside their specialness and returning to a child-like place of ordinary play, contentment and sorrow.

Others identify with the negative elements of their own personalities. They stand below their true space, seeing themselves as powerful, dangerous and destructive. But they often act compliantly, hoping by tremendous effort to hold in their own violence and anger. Such people often turn to prayer in hope of assuaging their dreadful sense of guilt. But, too often, they find themselves praying to a God who is as violent and cruel as they believe themselves to be.

It is hard for such people to find the courage to stand up to God, to take delight in themselves and their bodies, to be still without the fear of destruction. It takes effort to keep the forces of darkness at bay, and such people are often notoriously committed to goodness, with a corresponding terror of play and empty space.

Others experience themselves as a succession of different images, part-selves, which come and go and only partially relate to each other. I remember talking to a famous actress whom I once directed in some readings for radio. She was a believer who cared deeply about spiritual and personal integrity. She wanted to pray but found it difficult because it made her feel self-conscious. This was a painful experience. Normally she had very little consciousness of being an individual person. She poured herself into the parts she played, and wasn't sure, in prayer, which role she should adopt.

It is possible to know something of all these states, without being unusually neurotic or psychologically ill. So perhaps before we can stand still in our own space we need to be able to play, to experiment with trust, to revisit some of our childhood experiences, perhaps even to play hide-and-seek with God. One game of trust which toddlers play is the peek-a-boo game. You can only do this with someone else. You cover your eyes with your hands and then peek out to see if the other person is still there. You only do it because you know they are and you want to experiment with disappearing. Can you still be seen when you cannot see? Is the other person still there when you cannot see them? Or you hide behind a piece of furniture and peek out laughing and waving your hands. Now I'm here. Now I'm not.

Some experiments in prayer, some attempts to 'stand still in your own space' need to be as simple, and fascinating and repetitive, as this. Only by risk and repetition will we learn if it is grace which holds us, whether divine love and desire really permeate our environment.

Roles and role-playing

Yet we are not toddlers pretending to disappear or to be snowflakes but adults with professional and domestic boundaries and responsibilities. These we have chosen. They are our roles, the images among which we move and act in the world. Sometimes our roles express us, and come close to our sense of self. Sometimes they inhibit us, and we experience them as constraints and burdens.

We are spouses and parents and children, actors and ministers and servants and technicians, thinkers and doers and teachers and learners. The labels we wear express us truthfully, but they also inevitably frustrate and deny us.

One of the problems is that it is difficult to be honest about the frustration and denial. Being believers makes this worse. The Church is in trouble, as it always is, and so are many of the human values that faith cherishes. Christians who want to have some power and influence in the Church need to be strong and shrewd, and even guarded and defensive, in order to survive. The gospels are right to warn us about the penalties of power, but the Church has absorbed these warnings hypocritically. So there is much preaching of God's preference for the poor, much denunciation of the world of power and money by those who return to clean shirts, cooked meals and big houses, provided always by someone else. The true penalties of power are not only risked, but paid, by everyone who exercises power. Paying the penalty is a true experience of learning, an exercise of selfhood which puts our true self most at risk.

Those who hold power in the Church of God are in constant personal spiritual danger because they are forced to live, having given their consent, as images, icons. They easily lose touch with themselves as true selves and poor sinners. Yet this is how it is. For example, if you belong to the clergy and you are going to survive you have to become a bit of a manipulator. You have to know how to handle the bishop, the press, local pressure groups, religious enthusiasts of various kinds, well-meaning organisations, endless difficult and anxious people who demand or require time. After a few years of this, you start becoming sceptical of people's motives. That scepticism can easily turn into a joyless cynicism as you reflect on the cost of having become an icon.

With such demands upon you (and they are paralleled in other walks of life) you know that it is not prudent to be completely frank with anyone. Any personal unhappiness or guilt that you may experience is better kept as your own affair. Any passions must be kept absolutely secret. The world loves stories of wicked, dangerous, or simply over-sexed vicars, and has its own interests in keeping you on your pedestal until such time as you can be enjoyably or vengefully knocked off it. So, you will find, codes of conduct are laid down for you, and you won't survive unless you learn the rules. The space in which you live and move and have your being is quite narrow, controlled, and in certain important ways unreal.

Yet the Church lives on gossip, the power is in secrets withheld and divulged. I have sometimes gloomily compared my life as a television producer with my life as a priest. The part of the Church that I know, the Church of England, is a pompous and self-important organisation, which hides its depression under a veneer of polite, civilised concern. Its theology is fair-minded and honest, but its spirituality is superficial because it won't let itself address the dark questions of existence. They are kept in obscurity, along with the rest of the slime and the scandals.

The world of television was a rough house. There was a greed for power and control. There was plenty of verbal and emotional aggression. Yet I also found there an enormous sense of life and fun, creativity, energy and loyalty. In a strange way people were more transparent to one another, they did not feel they had to be good all the time or that they had to hide their anger or disappointment. The Church is too often a world of the nice and the good.

No one ever pretended that television was the kingdom of heaven. We knew it was a bear garden and that we were lucky to be alive. There are secrets and danger in every living environment. I have come to think that I slightly prefer danger to secrets, though I know something about both, and dread the power of both. Nevertheless most of the time there is enough concern, enough predictability, enough love around to make life worth living. Danger and secrets do not have to have the last word.

Praying with boundaries and space

So to go back to the beginning and to pray with this text. On the second day of creation God hollows out a great space. To create you God makes space and sets boundaries in the watery sea of human possibility. Your parents made you happen. You were conceived in a particular sexual act, and your genetic pattern was laid down without you having any conscious awareness of yourself as a unique human individual:

> ... didn't you and Mammy make me
> and God made the thread?[2]

You were born into this world at a particular time and place, and you have been patterned for existence by the care and love you received as a baby. In some respects you have had very little choice in the matter of who you are though, from your first moments, you have been contributing yourself to yourself, working out your own meaning within the space and boundaries set by providence. There is your blue dome, the sky above your head. There is the space for you to grow in. You are not to grow in anyone's space but your own, within the true horizons of what is given in your creation.

It is possible that for most of your life recently you have been strong and guarded both in the outer world and in your inner life. As always, there has been an awful lot to do. You have been acting from your strengths, buttressed, perhaps by some well-maintained defences, against your weaknesses.

True growth involves being willing to lay aside some of this armour and letting some of your buried life out into the sunlight. Bits of you are mature, bits of you are strong. But sometimes those bits are maintaining their strength at the expense of the rest of you. Let the armour become detachable.

Try to make time to listen, not only to the loud and confident bits of you, but to the poor and weak members of your own inner household. Listen to the crying infants and the adventurous toddlers who are struggling to balance and the five-year-olds who are learning to dance. I do believe that it is the poor and weak who will bring you to heaven, to the

[2] From Seamus Heaney, 'Catherine's Poem' in *The Island of the Children*, comp. Angela Huth, Orchard Books, 1987.

horizon's end, where the sun of God's promise meets the sea of God's possibilities.

Who are the weak and poor of your own household? Only you know. Perhaps it is your body that needs to be cherished. Perhaps the life of the senses is starved and confined. Perhaps it is the intellect which is longing to grasp and soar towards the light. Perhaps it is the mystical and intuitive side of yourself that is gasping for space. Perhaps it is your emotions that are tired, withered and dried up.

God is creating the whole of you. Not just the bits you choose to own, or the bits you like and admire. It is the weak and the poor who need your attention, who need special nurturing space to grow in. They in their turn will guide you to God, for the little ones always know how to trust when they sense the presence of deep and unconditional love.

That is why Christianity must learn about personal growth, and why it must not stop there. If we absorb the lessons of our inner journey we will realise that we are not complete in ourselves, that we continue to need others to bring us to maturity. We are made to contribute to the whole human environment, and we can and must do this, if we are to live. Here, as in the single personality, the strong and the weak need each other. The damaged and the wounded are as essential as the whole and the mature. Some people have had terrible emotional problems to deal with. They have been brought up in an atmosphere of cold neglect and indifference and have almost no capacity for relationship. Yet such people often have a gift of second sight, an extraordinary capacity for truth which is somehow bound up with their affliction. The psychiatrist Donald Winnicott said that he felt humble in the presence of schizoid persons because, for them, 'wicked means anything false, like being alive because of compliance'.[3] He believed that deeply fractured persons often saw things with a special clarity. The Bible would seem to endorse this. Some of the most gifted of God's prophets seem to have been afflicted with deep-rooted emotional disorders.

God is not judgemental. God creates order, rhythm, boundary and space, but he does not disown or deny disorder,

---

[3] Quoted from an unpublished talk on 'The Absence of a Sense of Guilt', 1966. See *Boundary and Space*, op. cit. p. 61.

disruption, darkness and night. He simply invites us to review ourselves, to see again, to be renewed and to be redeemed in the attempt to stand still in our own space.

God speaks in the space. You are also the space where God speaks. Through you, God is speaking to the universe a word that could not be said without you. God has a profound respect for you in your wholeness and your complexity. He seeks your true self because that is what he is giving you. God is not seduced by false images. He will turn you from the false by accidents, disasters, tragedies and jokes. This is his judgement. He will turn you aside from preoccupation with your image by means of a ludicrous spectacle, like a burning bush or an image of toddlers dancing on the radio. He comes as a glint on your path, as wild children hiding in the wood.

> Go, said the bird, for the leaves were full of children,
> Hidden excitedly, containing laughter.[4]

The space that you are in now is where you engage with the one Gerard Hughes has famously called 'the God of surprises' – here and nowhere else.

So stand before God. To stand is to stand up. However weak you feel, however weak you are, there comes a point when God requires you to stand up for yourself. Even Job, after all his sufferings, was commanded to stand his ground before the Holy One: 'Then the Lord answered Job out of the whirlwind: "Gird up your loins like a man; I will question you, and you declare to me"' (Job 40:6–7).

So stand still with your wounds and your damage and your weapons and all the baggage of your life. Flawed as you are you stand on holy ground. Your life so far is the earth you stand on, upright to heaven. This is the ground that God has cleared for you. Moses stood and faced God on desert ground. He was a fugitive from the murder of his youth, exiled and in danger. There was blood on the ground, blood on his hands. He knew that he had killed and could kill again. Yet there was the place he had to face God. This was the holy ground, the burning ground. The space between earth and heaven.

This is the blessed space, the space that God the creator

---

[4] From T. S. Eliot, 'Burnt Norton', the first of his *Four Quartets*.

hollows out for you, the place where his word is spoken and heard, a space which neither darkness nor chaos can finally overwhelm. God meets you here, and nowhere else.

Summary

On the second day God creates a firmament. I interpret this in terms of boundaries and space. By faith we can see God's order in the construction of our space-time universe, and in the planetary environment which has allowed for the evolution of life.

Because each one of us is a microcosmic universe we can see the same kind of ordering in the development of our personalities. We need to find out where we are in our development. We reflect on how healthy human growth comes about. We all need to be held secure, and we all need room to grow.

Experiments with prayer can help us trace both our growth into selfhood and the accidents which have disturbed the process. As praying adults we still need boundaries and space. We reflect on the social and religious environment which now sustains us. Or does it inhibit us?

The challenge to our prayer is to stand in our own space and know that it is the place where God meets us.

Suggestions for prayer

1   Read the passage from Genesis slowly to yourself. Then spend some time being aware of the space you are in. Notice the position of your body. Be particularly aware of what you are sitting or standing on. Try to just *be*. Notice what makes this difficult, and what helps.
2   Walk slowly around a part or the whole of your living or working space. Try to sense its dimensions, and notice the way in which you have used or filled your space to reveal, or conceal who you are. If it helps, try saying some of the words of Psalm 48:12–14: 'Walk about Zion, go all around it, count its towers, consider well its ramparts, go through its citadels; that you may tell the next generation that this is God, our God for ever and ever. He will be our guide for ever.'

3   Go outside at a quiet time of day or night when you can be
    alone. Stand on the ground and be aware of the sky.
    Breathe the air and spend some time just being aware of
    being held in life. Notice what happens to your body and
    to your thoughts and feelings.

4   Read the story of Moses' encounter with God at the
    burning bush (Exod. 3:1–6). What are the things in your
    life which might make you 'afraid to look at God' (v. 6)?

5   Staying with the story of Moses, be quiet with yourself for
    a few minutes and then say your own name repeatedly to
    yourself. As you do so, think of God calling your name in
    the depths of your being.

6   Try a drawing or painting prayer. Make a picture of the
    environment that you would most like to live in. Before
    you begin pray that God will show you something new
    about yourself that will be creative in your life. When you
    have finished, reflect for a while on what you have made,
    and consider what it shows you about yourself.

7   Read 1 Samuel 3:1–19. Imagine God calling you by name,
    as he called Samuel. Try the prayer of saying your name
    quietly to yourself and hearing God's voice in the depths of
    your being. Then try making your own response to God,
    either in Samuel's words ('Here I am') or in words of your
    own.

Day Three

The Green Gift

And God said, 'Let the waters under the sky be gathered together into one place, and let the dry land appear.' And it was so. God called the dry land Earth, and the waters that were gathered together he called Seas. And God saw that it was good. Then God said, 'Let the earth put forth vegetation: plants yielding seed, and fruit trees of every kind on earth bearing fruit with the seed in it.' And it was so. The earth brought forth vegetation: plants yielding seed of every kind, and trees of every kind bearing fruit with the seed in it, each according to its kind. And God saw that it was good. And there was evening and there was morning, the third day. (Gen. 1:9–13)

On the third day God sweeps aside the waters under the dome of heaven, and permits the dry land to bring forth life.

Patterns in glass and stone

Circles and petals, squares, triangles and hexagons, rose clusters, leaves and rays, shells and ovals, whorls and indented rectangles. Such patterns are frequently seen in sacred buildings; Hindu temples, mosques and cathedrals. Though these are not all natural shapes; they mimic nature, forming a kind of architectural calligraphy. This is perhaps most obvious in the art of Islam, where figurative representation is forbidden. What *is* allowed is *pattern*. The patterns that are woven into Persian and Turkish carpets or carved into the windows and ledges and pillars of mosques are like Arabic script, sacred writing. In Western Christendom this kind of patterning is found both in stone and glass. Colour and light, texture and pattern, number, shape will hint at the wholeness and interconnectedness of the created universe.

Some time ago I visited the cathedral at Chartres. It was a dark cold day in spring. At first the great windows seemed enormous, vague and gloomy. It took some time of wandering and staring before the structure became comprehensible and, as it were, began to sing. As I looked I began to find a vast, living medieval city of men and women. All had their place within the great cathedral, within the great body of glass and stone. Kings and prophets, angels and devils, young men, old women and children. The Mother of God looks out from the inner centre of the north rose window; Christ the King of the age to come sits enthroned at the heart of the south rose. In the west rose the Son of Man is seated in judgement. The three great spheres tell of time as well as space. Christ is the heart of the universe, of the past, present and future. Within this sacred geometry of time and space we are to find the meaning of our own existence.

So along the nave from east to west the glittering panels of glass portray the great themes of faith. The glass is a treasure house and those who paid for it expected to see themselves there. So the roses contain the coats of arms of the rich and the great, the panels show the traders and craftsmen at their normal occupations. Nobody was startled if the baker's face appeared as a saint or if a local lunatic's features were distorted to form a demon. It was a world where cruelty and comedy often went together.

The medieval glass masters were expressing something that was at the same time deep and obvious. Everything belonged together, bound by the dancing solidity of the stone and the colours and shapes of the glass. So they presented the unity of creation. They recognised the life given by the Creator pulsing through the fibres of all living matter. Seashells and flower patterns, spheres and spirals and squares. They *knew*, perhaps more through the geometry of mysticism than the sober findings of science, that the same simple patterns can be discerned again and again in all living forms. Beauty, simplicity, elegance and truth were obvious to them in the living world which they perceived. They rejoiced in the wisdom of the Creator. They knew that they lived in a more than human world. The geometric shapes and patterns, clear specks and rays of coloured glass penetrating the darkness, stood for the unknown physical and psychic laws on which God's universe is built. The glass masters knew, in a way that we do not know, the boundaries and spaces of the universe. They recognised that the Creator had mysteries and that there was much that they could not understand. But what they could understand they showed. Stars and angels, intelligences and the beasts of the field, beggars and scholars, hermits, poets and squalling babies. They could see the universe as an intelligible whole, structured by agencies visible and invisible under the direct command of God. Perhaps human beings have never been more confident that they had access to the mystery of life.

It is a confidence that we have found, and lost and found again, and the last finding is within living memory. In churches, cathedrals, colleges and chapels stained glass is still used to mediate the complexity and interconnectedness of the universe, displaying light and dark as the two sides of creation, an ordered whole, teeming with potential.

The human story of DNA

In 1953 Francis Crick and James Watson discovered the structure of the DNA molecule. They found out the mechanism by which living cells replicate themselves. In doing so they revolutionised the science of biochemistry and won themselves the Nobel Prize. James Watson was only twenty-four.

What they discovered was the austere and simple truth of the double helix. The DNA molecule consists of two helical chains twined round each other, with the base of each strand paired to a different base in the other. The secret of life is in the way this structure replicates itself. The two strands peel apart and each one becomes the template on which a new strand is constructed, so becoming a new double helix. The new dual strand is, of course, an exact copy of the original. The solution to the problem of life which Watson and Crick proposes is elegant, simple, economical and ingenious. In 1968 Watson did something rather unusual for a respected member of the scientific community. At the invitation of Lawrence Bragg, the director of the Cavendish Laboratory in Cambridge, he wrote a personal account of the discovery. Scientists, when they write about their triumphs, often adopt a cool and impersonal style as if the facts and conclusions they wish to present would be contaminated if they were to tell too much of the human side of the story.

But *The Double Helix* is a deliberately gossipy account. James Watson believed that the more objective approach 'would fail to convey the spirit of an adventure characterised both by youthful arrogance and by the belief that the truth, once found, would be simple as well as pretty'.[1]

There *is* arrogance in this account, but it is the arrogance of a man who has achieved his life's goal at an incredibly young age and has left more experienced rivals gasping. It is a lively story, but not particularly tactful. Take the author's portrait of his colleague Francis Crick. Crick comes across as immodest, loud, endlessly talkative, with an appalling laugh. Watson lets us know that many of his contemporaries found him rather odious. He is just as unsparing of himself. We get a picture of a clever young American who messed up his research fellowship, a self-confessed failure at chemistry who once ignited a laboratory by heating benzene over a Bunsen burner. Most of the time he is more interested in sex. So, Watson says, we two who discovered the secret of life were neither saints nor geniuses.

Neither Watson nor Crick had any time for religion, dismissing it as a mistake of the past. The world they lived in was a mixture of English stuffiness and formality, with the undertones of gossip, vanity, competition, crudity, fun and nonsense. Watson knows, in his account, that this environment played a part in firing them to success. It provided the edge, the resistance, the human jungle of ambition, energy and envy. Of course the Cavendish pair worked hard. There were hours of frustration, hours of patient research and calculation. There were moments of disappointment and defeat. There were lucky guesses. There were sudden hunches and intuitions which proved mostly wrong but sometimes right. There were earnest lunches in the Eagle pub, wine parties and outings. What is clear from the account is that the scientists who hit the jackpot really enjoyed *each other*. They were friends, but almost more important than that, they were fellow-conspirators. They played and boasted. And the play came into the work. It was serious play. They played with molecular models,

---

[1] James D. Watson, *The Double Helix*, Penguin, 1968.

coloured spheres and rods that are not unlike the toys of pre-school children. When they got bored they talked about sex, and shared academic gossip. Crick never read a newspaper but knew the contents of his wife's *Vogue*.

Watson is as frank about his rivals as he is about his friends. Linus Pauling, a great chemist who was racing to solve the problem in America, is portrayed as a wizard, a brilliant manipulator of words and concepts, too clever and too scheming to make the final breakthrough. Maurice Wilkins, the bachelor physicist who switched to biology because of the ethical problems of atomic research, comes across as nervous, buttoned-up. He is unhappy in his own laboratory and creeps off to Cambridge to gossip with Crick and Watson, and to moan about his gifted colleague Rosalind Franklin, who is making his life a misery. Rosalind Franklin herself is a truly tragic character. Watson, true to form, portrays her as a negative, cold woman whose contribution to the discovery was almost entirely obstructive. She is, for Watson, almost a bad witch. He has no sympathy for her, but speculates, like a critical adolescent schoolboy, on what she would look like if she wore make-up and did something about her hair. Yet Rosalind Franklin came very close to solving the problem. Francis Crick eventually admitted that he and Watson would never have built the successful model of the double helix without having access to her photographic research. It is now thought that she was betrayed by Wilkins, who showed one of her key photographs to her rivals. It was Franklin's fate to be exploited and discarded in the race for the secret of life, and only more recently has this dark lady of DNA been recognised as a great scientist in her own right.

Rosalind Franklin was, in fact, a very traditional dedicated scientist. She was rigorously methodical, cool and logical in her approach. She exhibited all the so-called 'masculine' virtues of rationality. In contrast, Crick and Watson were much more erratic in their working patterns, much more in touch with emotion and intuition, the supposed properties of the feminine.

As I think about the fate of Rosalind Franklin I am reminded of the story of Jacob and Esau. She is, in a way, cheated of her birthright by a clever younger brother, who succeeds in part by guile. She was an honourable woman, a woman of duty. She may well have worked longer and harder than her rivals. She knew that her methods were not at fault. But she never had their luck. Perhaps what she missed was serendipity, starlight, the gift of play and laughter, and even a necessary streak of ruthlessness.

Patterns of life and death

What has this to do with the Genesis account? I believe that the story of the discovery of DNA reflects some of the qualities displayed by life itself as it spreads its green potential over the earth. Life is greedy, life is selfish. Life envies and is envied. The sheer ruthlessness of the way life swarms and squirms across the planet can provoke a human reaction of disgust. Wriggling maggots, writhing snakes, teeming ants and locusts, even the way clusters of sharp green shoots thrust themselves up into the air, as shown by speeded up photography, can make us feel slightly squeamish. What is this life that is so blindly desperate to grow, to feed off other life and then crumble and decay? Buddhist teachings interpret the cycle of life as endlessly fuelled by craving and aggression. Life is empty of the possibility of peace and satisfaction, unless it finds ways of transcending itself by the knowledge of death and dissolution.

The biblical view is less gloomy. It is on the third day that God creates life. Replication, multiplication, is a command of God, and God sees that it is good. Creation has prepared for this. First there was light. Then there was the creation of space, and the boundaried firmament, which is the womb of the future. Then, on the third day, life on earth.

From the biological point of view what makes life *life* is its mysterious power to replicate itself. Life is alive, and it is not only single but multiform, various, changing, dying and living again. Yet this is not so easy to live with and assimilate. Even within the Christian tradition there have been spiritual teachers who have lamented the necessity for physical reproduction and have sought comfort in the belief that the true self is purely spiritual. God, they believe, did not really *intend* the human body at all. But Christian orthodoxy has insisted both that creation is inherently good, and also that 'the Word became flesh'.

From our human perspective life gets ever more compli-cated. From simple inanimate forms life develops relentlessly in many different directions at once. *Our* bit of life has tri-umphed at consciousness and communication. We have made a journey from flesh to spirit. Yet we are still flesh, and the flesh that makes us talk and make love and replicate ourselves is God's creation. What lives also has the power to make alive. There is no life without the communication of life.

Multiplication is the name of the game. The mechanism of this replication was what Crick and Watson discovered. They knew that somewhere in the living cell was the secret. In every living cell was the coded power of new life 'something that knows ... something that doesn't die when you die'.[2]

The continuation of life depends on death and disintegra-tion. The code of life, locked in the DNA, can only create new forms by splitting and re-pairing. The individual cell dies to become two, and then the organism dies, and the genes are carried on. Death comes to transmit life.

Yet death is also like a necessary restraint on the ruthlessness of the life-force. Traditional Christian theology recognises this in balancing its doctrine of creation with its doctrines of the fall and original sin. These present death as a punishment for sin. Creation and the coming of death are separated out into two historic movements. The first reflects the creative splen-dour of God. The second describes the weakness and fallibility of human beings, which spreads out to infect the whole cre-ated order with violence.

It is less easy for us today to split death and life up into two distinct historic movements. Death seems to be given along with life, almost as the cost of it, and certainly as a necessary part of it. I think that the Christian doctrines of the fall and original sin are ways of intuiting the ruthlessness of life and the awesome need for death in a creative universe. The planet greens with organisms, but it has its own boundaries, set by God, which must be respected.

So we have to come to terms with the fact that life and death are twined together. Life is killing us, even as we live, and all at the same time, with a ruthless disregard for our

[2] From *Life Story*, William Nicholson's drama for BBC television, about Watson and Crick's discovery of the structure of DNA.

preference or convenience. Again and again life is sacrificed
for new life to be formed, for different life to flourish. Life and
sacrifice are the twin laws of the universe. They enfold us
physically, emotionally and spiritually.

How do we pray with these complex yet obvious truths?
First by recognising that our whole experience is entwined by
creativity and destruction. There is a necessary ruthlessness and
cruelty about the life-process, which we see in the story of the
gene, and the story of the scientists who discovered DNA, and
in the story of ourselves. Another scientist, Richard Dawkins,
in a popular book published in 1976 describes genes as 'selfish'.
The evolution of life is the story of a blind and desperate
conflict for survival. Genes are the only immortals, and they
build themselves carriers which will give them the best chance
of perpetuating themselves. All our agility and intelligence is at
the service of genes which neither think nor feel nor desire
nor fear.

The physical struggle for survival is carried on into our
social and emotional lives. Intelligence, strength, aggression,
drive and skill make for success in the human world. But
human beings are blessed and cursed with self-awareness, and
that includes knowledge of our own frailty. If we simply
imitate the blind ruthlessness of our genes we are more likely
to end up in prison or in a psychiatric ward than in fulfilment.
Human beings have knowledge of the death that awaits them,
and need to learn to die in order to be whole.

This is the great insight of Christian teaching, the gift that
Christ brought into the world in his own person. We are not
machines but wounded beings who need the lessons of our
humiliations. To go back to the story of the discovery of DNA
we can see that Watson and Crick won the race for the truth
of life at least in part because they were open to their own
immaturity and foolishness. They played, they despaired, they
drank wine, they built models like children. They were
humiliated, and they learnt from their humiliations. One of
the worst blows was when they thought they were on their
way to an answer and summoned Rosalind Franklin to view a
painstakingly-constructed model. She could see at a glance
that they had made a stupid miscalculation and made it clear to
them that her journey from London to Cambridge had been a
waste of time. Yet, after their initial disappointment Crick and

Watson got down to work again. They were flexible enough, crafty enough, to learn even from stupid errors.

Rosalind Franklin was a much more conventional scientist. She behaved like an observing machine, as far as she could, though this was not entirely natural to her. She was actually an impulsive woman, capable of fun, passion and delight in science and life. But her public face was serious, uncompromising and intolerant of weakness. While still a young woman she contracted cancer, and died at the age of thirty-seven. Yet, in her dying she displayed a heroism which moved her friends and colleagues. She faced her last illness with great courage and worked on at her research until a few weeks before the end. Even James Watson came to recognise a greatness in her.

Much could be said here about the differences between men and women and the difficulties for gifted women of her time in being accepted as equals in the world of men. Humiliation, ignorance and the knowledge of death must all be integrated into that quest for life which is specifically human.

Watson and Crick integrated weakness and playfulness in their way, and it led them to fame and glory. Rosalind Franklin did it in hers and it seems to have led her to a kind of wisdom. Both were acting out parables of human life greater than themselves, and yet in ways that were unique to themselves and their times. Even so, things could have been different. Rosalind Franklin might have grasped the truth about the double helix, and won the Nobel Prize. But she did not. After the event we cannot judge, we can only perceive.

The double helix is a beautiful structure and it is the pattern on which all life is ordered. This fascinates me because it reminds me of the patterns that I encounter in social, emotional and spiritual aspects of life. The twining together of two similar opposites, the unzipping of each half of the pattern's structure and the formation of a wholly new entity, identical in form to the original – you cannot help but be aware of the great drives of sex and self-transcendence and death. The biological mirrors the spiritual, and vice versa. Perhaps the artists who design stained glass should fill our cathedrals and churches with double helices!

Conflicts of life and death

More than that the double helix reminds me of other inter-twinings which are familiar from the spiritual traditions. Christianity knows, in its deep wisdom, that the way creation and death are locked together is both an embrace and a conflict, and that it is ever-fruitful:

> Death and life have contended
> in that combat stupendous:
> The prince of life who died
> reigns immortal. . .[3]

Christianity is the religion of the cross. It is biased towards death, and unlike its parent, Judaism, is always in danger of negating the goodness of life given by the Creator. It contains its scandal in careful balance with its promise of resurrection and eternal life.

Yet it will always be a hard faith. The emphasis on humility and death in Christian teaching is a contradiction of all that we naturally know about life. It contends with our necessary aggression, desire and ambition. And yet the promise is that those who live with a realistic knowledge of death are actually closer to life and the gift of it than those who deny and pretend about death. The promise also goes on that when death is allowed, in its due time and season, it is a creative annihilation which scatters the seeds of new life.

Seasons of the spirit

So in terms of our own lives we can pray inside the conflict of life and death as we experience it. There are seasons of the spirit, and some of the best fruit requires autumn pruning and winter dying. There is an art of relaxing into weakness and incapacity, a kind of 'negative capability' which, paradoxically, seems to help something new to germinate and grow.

Dying to live is both a law of the universe and a personal discovery. It is a spiritual challenge to endure 'dead' times in our own development for the sake of the life to come. There are real periods of 'decomposition' which have to be endured

---

[3] *Victimae Paschali*, Easter hymn ascribed to Wipo, eleventh century.

and survived if we are to live fully. Depression and anxiety are natural accompaniments to these transitions.

Many adolescents respond to the physical and mental turmoil of the teenage years by sleeping a lot and withdrawing from their families; becoming sullen and critical, and yet, at the same time being over-sensitive to any criticism levelled at them. You can almost *see* the inner struggle for a new self to be born. Facing the menopause or retirement can produce disorientation and symptoms of physical and psychological distress. These are natural and cultural rhythms; other times of apparent disintegration belong to the unique circumstances of our lives. Few would doubt though, that depression is increasingly common in our affluent and materialistic society. Part of this is in the high expectations many people have of what they can achieve and of that they ought to acquire in the way of property, wealth and security. The driven-ness of contemporary society means that it is difficult to have fallow periods. In academic life, and even in the Church, the gift of sabbatical leave is often hedged with expectations that some new skill will be achieved, some field of learning mastered, or a book researched, written and delivered. Without the fallow times, the 'rehearsals for death' which are part of life, it is impossible for new life to break through.

The Spirit of God is called the life-giver; the Spirit of God raises the crucified Jesus from the dead. In Christian tradition Christ is God's child, the start of a new creation. The life of Christ is passed on among us through the Word and the Spirit, through bread and wine and water. Christ is two- natured, twined as the double-helix is twined, man and God without confusion or separation. Christ the whole and the holy, the living and the sacrificed one, replicates his life in us. He multiplies among us, bringing the dead to life.

In this faith, dark as it is sometimes, we endure the dark of death. This is the decomposition of all that we are and have known ourselves to be. There is winter and summer, seed-time and harvest, and to live fully is to know death, to fear it and accept it, even with greeting, in its proper time.

At one time of emotional darkness and death the only way I could pray was with a stone. I held the stone in my hand and tried to still my body and calm my mind. The stone was cold in my hand, cold as death and peaceful. It soothed the

agitation of strained nerves and wild circling thoughts. It was a
solid thing to mould my hand around. As I sat with it, holding
on to it, letting my hand be moulded to its shape it gradually
grew warm. So I knew that there was new life in me, in the
simple act of warming a cold stone in my hand, and feeling the
warmth of my blood communicated back to me.

At another time I planted some seedlings of culinary herbs. I
had bought them in a packet from the National Trust and they
sat on my windowsill in little green plastic dishes. For days
they did nothing. And then one day I saw two or three tiny
shoots. At the time I so doubted my ability to give life, or to
nurture what was alive, that I expected them to die. I half
expected my own misery to infect them with a creeping desire
to die. Every morning I thought I would find them shrivelled
and dead, having sprung up violently out of their dishes in the
night and fallen exhausted into the sink! Yet they lived, basil
and thyme and sage, and cheered up my mealtimes for months
to come.

Although I knew it intellectually, it is because of such
experiences that I have come to believe that life itself is the
central miracle of our existence. This life is spiritual and
physical; I see both the DNA life and the sacrificial life of
Christ as coming from the wisdom and generosity of God our
Creator. I have come to think that our response to the gift of
life is the most serious and lovely challenge we shall ever
encounter, and that it takes the whole of each person's life and
death to discover how to respond appropriately.

I have also come to recognise something about violence and
ruthlessness. In the quest for life people often do dreadful
things. The life force is very strong in us, and it is planted in
our bodies and brains by God. To keep the gift of life most of
us will do anything. We will accept restrictions in losses of
limbs or eyesight or hearing, and adjust accordingly. In our
emotional development we will also strive for survival at
almost any cost. We will split off parts of ourselves, deny, lie
about and repress bad experiences. This is human. We will
fight and kill if we have to. In the quest for life some are hurt
to the point of acting out their injury in violence to others.

Religion is a civilizing force. Religious practice tends to
calm our more violent instincts, and religious teachings
encourage us to live in harmony with others and with

creation. But the mission of religion is in vain if it fails to recognise our primitive helplessness. Hurt people lash out, betray, feed off and envy each other. Life is greedy, life envies and is envied. The planet remains green, and green is the colour of the monster that longs in its envy to diminish and destroy. Every person's emotional life has its dark and unresolved areas. There are break-ups and walkings-out. There are cold deserts of withdrawal and indifference. There are gulfs of terror and anxiety that open up when people come close to each other's pain.

What is important is to recognise the cry for life which lies behind even the most destructive and despairing behaviour. It could be said that even violence is an abortive attempt at making a relationship.

By reflecting on this I have come to understand something of what forgiveness is, and could be. Sometimes forgiveness is presented as an act which displays a certain kind of moral superiority, a condescension by which the good excuse the less good. But forgiveness of that kind is nothing more than condescension. Real forgiveness springs, I believe, not from superiority, but from a deep recognition of our own poverty, fragility and desperate need. Forgiveness is possible when we see our own ruthlessness and guile, the primitive hate and envy which we have incorporated, and may have denied in order to survive. Forgiveness is possible when we begin to learn to be gentle and humble with ourselves, to nurture both the wild and the wise life within us, to care for our own needs with the tenderness that comes from self-knowledge. Failure is a preparation for forgiveness, a knowledge of death which can bring us to live with wisdom.

As Christians it is our life to seek Christ, and to allow his life to be replicated in us. We come to Christ using our intelligence and perception, our strengths of mind and body, by calculation, intuition and starlight we come, as the Magi did – those practitioners of an old and dark science. We come through the night to the place where he is born for us. He is the new child of our desire, the child of the God of life, and he lies helpless in Bethlehem, the house of bread. This is not merely a human city but a spiritual state, a waste place, a transition on the edge of existence.

All are allowed here, though it is home for no one. Yet it is where our journey leads to, a place where the fool and the beast and the wise are gathered together in wonder. There are no disqualifications.

All can come, though not all want to. It is possible even for clergy and journalists, stockbrokers, politicians and academics, as long as they come not to control but to love, with their gifts and out of their poverty: 'In him was life, and the life was the light of all people' (John 1:4). Here too, come the poor and the failed, the immature and the depressed, the terrified and the disappointed. These are the ones who know their poverty, who have practised death for so long that it is life that is the surprise for them. Here is the place to acknowledge and lay down envy and exchange it for inclusion.

So, as you pray with the verses of Genesis which celebrate the greening of the planet, celebrate also in your heart the advent of Christ, our child, God's son, the two-natured of earth and heaven. He is weakness and strength, pity and power, mercy and truth, twined in endless embrace.

Come to him, as you pray, bringing your faith, green as any leaf.

Summary

On the third day God creates life. We know by intuition that all life is somehow bound up together. There is a sacred calligraphy in religious art which mirrors nature. The discovery of the structure of DNA is spiritually momentous because it shows us what life's pattern is and how it works. We reflect on the human story of the discovery of DNA as a parable of the paradoxical qualities of life.

Then we consider how death and life are related in Christian theology. Death is a necessity in an evolving universe, and this insight must permeate our spirituality. We reflect again on the DNA story and the clues it gives about learning from our humiliations.

The challenge for our prayers is to become aware of how death and life are at work within us. We need to be aware of the different seasons of the spirit. Here Christ, the two-natured, is the focus of our faith and understanding.

Suggestions for prayer

1 Read the passage from Genesis slowly to yourself. Think about the mystery of life and the capacity of living forms to replicate themselves. Notice your feelings and thoughts at being a part of this great pattern.

2 Position yourself so that you can see a tree or a flower or a plant. Touch it if you can. Try to realise that every cell in your body is made up of the same sort of stuff. What does this make you think or feel? What responsibility does it give us for the care of our planet?

3 Be as still as you can and pray with two phrases, one reminding you of the creation life, the other of the life Christ brings into the world. You could try 'the gift of life' and 'the life of Christ'. Try to experience where these realities meet and conflict in your life.

4 Think about your parents, who gave you life, and about your own children, if you have them. Greet them one by one, by name. What does it mean to you to be part of a chain of life, a gene-carrier? Be open to all your reactions, negative and positive.

5 Think of the circumstances in which your own physical or emotional life was most threatened or damaged. What do you want to say to the people who were involved in a negative way? What do you want to say to God about them?

6 Think of any person whose physical or emotional life you have damaged, or for whom you have felt green-eyed envy. What have you learnt from the experience? Bring your thoughts and feelings to God.

7 Read John 1:1–5. Try to think or feel the areas in your own life which need to be illuminated by the true light of Christ's life. Write down the word LIFE on a piece of paper. Then write down all the other words and phrases which come into your head and make that a basis for your prayers.

Day Four

The Cosmic Calendar

And God said, 'Let there be lights in the dome of the sky to separate the day from the night; and let them be for signs and for seasons and for days and for years, and let them be lights in the dome of the sky to give light upon the earth.' And it was so. God made the two great lights – the greater light to rule the day and the lesser light to rule the night – and the stars. And God set them in the dome of the sky to give light upon the earth, to rule over the day and over the night, and to separate the light from the darkness. And God saw that it was good. And there was evening and there was morning, the fourth day. (Gen. 1:14–19)

On the fourth day God creates the stars, the sun and the moon. They are made to mark time for us, to provide a cosmic calendar. God intends us to be aware of time. Through the solar and lunar cycles we know of birth days and death days. All the anniversaries of our experiences are signed for us by the movements of the heavenly bodies. We calculate, we remember, we live, we hand on the significant moments. Because the ability to measure time is one of the gifts of creation we can deduce that God honours history. God remembers.

Sacred memories
Again and again the scriptures call on God's people to 'remember'. They are to remember the greatness and the mercy of God, and they are to remember their own fragility. In this memory is security for the present time and hope for the future. If they forget the otherness of God and try to invent their own identity they will lose security in the present

and will be able to look on the future only with despair: 'Your life shall hang in doubt before you; night and day you shall be in dread, with no assurance of your life' (Deut. 28:66). Time itself will become a hideous burden: 'In the morning you shall say, "if only it were evening!" and at evening you shall say, "if only it were morning!" – because of the dread that your heart shall feel' (v.67).

The stars have another meaning in God's universe. They stand for abundance and prosperity. God promises Abraham that his descendants will be as numerous as the stars of heaven or the sand on the seashore (Gen. 22:17). The promised leader of the nations is seen as a star (Num. 24:17) rising from the line of Jacob. Yet the stars are also dangerous. Because they are mysterious, yet visible, they can seduce the human heart to idolatry:

> And when you look up to the heavens and see the sun, the moon and the stars, all the host of heaven, do not be led astray and bow down to them and serve them, things that the Lord your God has allotted to all the peoples every-where under heaven. (Deut. 4:19)

God's people are always tempted to mistake things for God, to reduce the tension between the Creator and the creation. Though the stars may look eternal they are themselves crea-tures of time; they wheel and change, burn out, die and come to birth. Only God is deathless.

Unlike God we live in time. Time is what makes created things different from God. It is important to realise how ser-iously the Bible takes time because religion sometimes seems to offer an *escape* from time. Religion often invests in the idea that there is a timeless bit of us, which relates exclusively to a timeless God. This bit of us is often thought of as mysteriously invulnerable to change and death. The Genesis account of creation has no room for such comforting ideas. Before *we* come into existence at all time is created, and time is one of the conditions of life on earth. A condition, and also a restraint.

But time is also freedom. What happens in time, really happens. It is history. What happens in time is real. It marks us, and enables us to make our mark, to write our own signature against our patch of reality. Time makes us accountable. The freedom to act and be acted on in time is part of the freedom God desires for us. Time means change. Nothing is fixed. We are not predetermined. Our destiny is not 'written in the stars'. But the stars do remind us of what has been done to us and what we have done.

We write our meaning into the stars that wheel above us. We constellate the universe by the meanings we attach to what happens in time. And God honours this process of making meaning. Our writing in the sky is open to God's grace and judgement. Time is real to God, as real as it is to us. God remembers our times. We can say with the Psalmist, 'My times are in your hand' (Ps. 31:15). Yet this is still hard for us to accept. Christian theology tells us that God is eternal and changeless. This immutability in God is often presented as part of God's perfection. *We* are mortal, ever subject to accident, change and death. But God is changeless and immortal. So to become like God we must progress towards fixity, change-lessness, stability. Time itself has been seen as a symptom of human imperfection, and the eternity of God as a contra-diction and denial of the reality of time. The Christian Church has attempted to devise forms of spirituality which have tried to make people invulnerable to time. Death was seen as the perfection to strive towards because in death we are past change. Life was dangerous, a sea of temptation. It was a major task of spirituality to eradicate stimulation. Desire was suspect, so was laughter, so was anything which cracked the shell of control. To reach God you had to renounce the limitations of time.

But time is not only limitation, it is opportunity. The sharpest minds in Christendom have always pressed us to acknowledge the gracious truth that we are not God, we are God's creatures, time-bound and limited. Perfection comes, not through an imitation of fixity but by being willing to be subjected to process. We must be marked by time, schooled and battered by time in order to grow into the likeness of God. Time is our playpen, and while we are alive we are not ready for eternity. While we live we really do inhabit history. We are grounded in particularity, and it is here that God meets us, and not anywhere else. It is a bogus spirituality which bases itself on the belief that there is an eternal bit of us, free from the pressures of time. Intellectually and theologically we may recognise this, but it is still hard to accept. We hanker for immortality, on our terms.

Our problem with time reveals itself in the reluctance we have to face old age. Women in particular come to dread the truth revealed by the mirror. Skin and hair age and change, and there is little we can do. I had a shock when I had a new passport photograph taken, and found for the first time that I could see in my face not only my mother's features, but my grandmother's! I had never seen it before, but there it was. She is dead, and yet I bear the marks of her in my face. I never thought I resembled my father, who was tall and strong, athletic and bald. But as I have grown older, I have found his freckles on my arms. They were always there, I just failed to notice that they were his! Since his death some years ago I have found it strange and moving to carry these marks of his on through time.

We should like to have control of time, to make *our* mark on time, and some of us do manage to a bit. But on the whole time marks us more than we mark it.

When my marriage ended one of the things I did to fill in time was to knit. I wasn't good at it, but it was soothing. It gave me a kind of satisfaction to knit up the rolls and rolls of wool, to make them into pieces of something else. I also learnt something about rage. I was not very patient, or very skilled, and I often went badly wrong. I had to ask people for help, and that made me feel more in touch with people at a time when I could have felt very isolated. The knitting was a kind of serious joke. But it also drove me mad. I remember one desperate afternoon when I discovered that I had used the wrong colour for a couple of stitches forty rows back. I could have ignored it, but it was an obvious mistake, and I knew that I could not live with it. It looked wrong. As I began to undo it I felt almost overcome with anger and disgust. I found that I was almost tearing the garment to pieces in my fury to undo the mistake. The wool seemed resistant, as if it had acquired a sulky perversity all of its own. I could not stop until I had unravelled the wool to a point before the mistake occurred. Even then I found it hard to stop. I had become used to the passion of destruction. The garment, now somewhat humbled and shrunken, could be reworked. The floor was by now covered in twisted wool. I could see how much violence and self-disgust I had projected on to the knitting. It sounds absurd, but the knitting had become a sign for me of the mistakes of time, and it called out an almost volcanic rage from the depths of my being. I had to tear it apart, violently, in order to start again.

Healing the wounds of time

What does such violence mean? Time, it seems, does not heal. It wounds and destroys, and leaves us with deeds done which we want undone, opportunities missed which will not come again.

The diary and the calendar, based on the heavenly clock-faces of the moon and the sun and the stars, remind us of what time has done to us, and of what we have done to time. They are the constellations of the real, physical universe. Their movements can be measured and universally agreed.

But the external universe which eyes and telescopes can scan has its internal, personal counterpart. This is the universe which is constellated by our first experiments in awareness. When you see a baby looking up into the face of its mother or father, fascinated, puckering its own face into little scowls and laughs, reaching up to touch the other face, you are seeing a universe being set with stars. The adults mirror back the baby to itself, passing unspoken messages of love, security, anxiety, delight, hostility or indifference. These are the feelings and meanings which constellate the child's universe; the fixed points which give us hope and unrest all our life long.

These perceptions about the importance of early experience are not new. They are present in mythology and folk-tale, and, of course, in the sagas and narratives of the Bible.

Joseph

One of the most powerful sagas in the Old Testament is the story of Joseph. Joseph was the favourite child of the patriarch Jacob. Joseph dreamed two dreams which perfectly expressed the place in the universe which his father's favouritism had assigned to him. In one, he was the chief corn-sheaf, to which the lesser sheaves bowed down. In the other, even more revealing dream, he was the very centre of the universe. The sun, moon and eleven stars all bowed down before him. To his brothers, the meaning was clear. Joseph was setting himself up above father, mother and the eleven of them. This was enough to arouse them to murderous rage, and they plotted his removal. They did not actually kill him, but they acted out his murder, they murdered their image of him, and brought bloody garments back to his father.

Joseph was lucky. He was preserved and taken off to Egypt as a slave. It was as though the proud, dangerous universe in which he had been living was transformed by real danger. His specialness was transformed by the experience of degradation. In this he encountered the true God of the stars, the God of heaven, who turned his precociousness into deep wisdom. So, in time, the wounds of time were healed in Joseph and he became a great prophet in a foreign land.

Looking at the development of the story we can see the ambiguity of Joseph's original dreams. They were double-edged signs. They did tell truly of his future greatness. But they also acted as the catalyst which brought about the humiliation he needed. He was a perfectly horrible child, not through his own fault, and it took real horror to save him.

The fascinating thing about the story is that at the very moment when his brothers come seeking him as the great power in Egypt he reverts to his childhood behaviour. The brothers do not know who he really is. Joseph, for the first time in his life, has real power over them. And he cannot resist it. In their presence he only knows how to be the special, precocious child. He hides his true identity, just as it was once effectively hidden by the coat of many colours. Then he plays a savage trick on his brothers, as nasty, if less lethal, than the trick they played on him. Yet, this time, he takes no pleasure in it. He does not boast, he weeps. His specialness no longer gives him the illusion of protection from insult. I like to think that at this point in the narrative (Gen. 42:24) the wounds of time are very close to the surface and Joseph is in mourning. Perhaps he mourns for his lost identity. He mourns that he has always had to be special and never just himself. He mourns that he has been the favourite, and that he has been hated and envied, without his true self being allowed to live. He has lived from power, from charisma, from his good looks and intelligence, and in return he has been haunted by the fear and jealousy of others.

The breakthrough for Joseph is the moment when he tears off his mask and confesses, 'I am your brother Joseph'. Even then he has to say it twice before his brothers can respond to him (Gen. 45:1–4). They do not know him now because they have never known him. All they have known is his image, and his image is what they murdered. So they are full of confusion and guilt.

But the end of the story, like the end of all good stories, is of weeping and reconciliation. The wounds of time are acknowledged and transformed, so that they become an integral part of a truer, more fruitful relationship.

Time, truth and forgiveness

Time does not only wound and destroy. It is also where truth is unravelled and made accessible. When I attacked my knitting I was half aware of being in touch with an inner rage about the past and the mistakes I had made. I wanted to go back and find the mistake, the moment at which I had misread the pattern. Sitting on the floor surrounded by discarded wool I felt both frustrated and cleansed. It was a real effort to knit the wool up again, to turn from despair and do the task that was needed. Since I have become a priest I have seen this kind of pattern happen many times in people's lives. There is an unravelling which has to happen in its own time and its own way, and then there is sometimes volcanic rage and sorrow, or deep despair, and then the slow turning to the obvious, necessary tasks of reparation, which are not necessarily dramatic, but gentle, humble and patient.

It is hard for us to heal the mistakes of time because we live in an instant world, and one which has its own secular investment in denying time. Time is apportioned unfairly, like money. The successful executives leave for work on commuter trains before dawn and return, exhausted, after dark. Yet time hangs like a millstone round the necks of those without work, and those who are old or sick.

I hate rush and panic, and yet I work in a world which seems to thrive on the excitement of not having enough time.

Deadlines are a stimulus to action. I live in fear that if I had the time I really feel I need, I would never do anything at all!

Time is where we hurt, and we are not at ease in it. Either there is too little or too much. Time is what reminds us constantly of our creaturely status. We are made of dust and doomed to die. The knowledge of this, and the memory of past wounding constitute the oppression of time.

To escape, we trivialise. We have a preference for bland and instant communication. The anniversary is kept or forgotten, but it often passes without true warmth. The joke, the extravagance, the forgotten, conventional or unwanted gift are substitutes for memory. Memory is dangerous because it always contains pain. And when it comes to the past we conceal with laughter what we dare not reveal in tears.

This inability to remember the wounds of time makes people shallow and hollow inside. They become past masters of denial. They simply press the 'erase' button when anything painful gets too close. They know that it is not cool to cling, not strong to feel dependence or need of another human being. Everything, every relationship, every desire is dispensable and replaceable. In this way they deny time and the wounds of time. They act on the world from a place of invulnerability, defended by their incapacity for feeling.

I have sometimes envied such people, and yet in my heart I know the price they pay for their freedom from time. The price is emotional death; they cannot feel or change or mourn or die. And because of that their capacity for life is narrowed and sterilised. Such people are often found in the caring professions. They are priests, therapists, doctors, nuns. They are the promiscuous celibates who give themselves to no one, but break the hearts of others. Secretly they envy those they wound, because they know that the wounded are more alive than those who have no true capacity for suffering.

But what we forget, what we refuse to suffer, we are condemned to repeat. Memory is a holy gift, and God built it into the universe when he created the sun and moon and stars as signs of the seasons and years. The recovery of memory is essential for the healing of what time has hurt.

In Christianity the key to healing the wounds of time lies in the gift of forgiveness. But forgiveness is not straightforward. Many of the wounds which Christian people keep locked in their hearts are to do with past wrongs; either inflicted or suffered. They have been told that they should forgive, and yet forgiveness seems impossible. The prayer of Jesus, 'Forgive us our trespasses as we forgive those who trespass against us', brings a sense of oppression rather than comfort.

On the other hand Christians often become uncomfortable when they meet unforgiving attitudes. I have often heard murmured criticism from Christians about the way the Jewish community holds on to the memory of the holocaust. They feel that there is something distasteful about continuing to remind the world of this particular atrocity when there are other genocides in recent history which do not appear to be mourned so deeply. The Muslim community, in particular, has criticized the keeping of a special Holocaust Memorial Day. Why, some ask, cannot the Jewish community 'forgive and forget'? Yet I suspect the Christian frustration with the Jews comes from a deep and only partly acknowledged guilt in the Christian conscience. Jews see the holocaust as the logical culmination of centuries of Christian anti-Semitism. It is hard for Christians to accept that the seeds of anti-Semitism lie in their own New Testament; in St Matthew's ascription of blood guilt to the Jews (Matthew 27:25) for all generations, and to St John's relentless polemic against 'the Jews'. Historically, Christian rhetoric against the Jews has often been extremely vicious. Christians hate admitting all this, but it is true. When Christians then suggest that the Jews might forgive the Holocaust it is not surprising that Jewish people feel affronted. For it sounds as though Christians are saying that Jews should erase their *memories*. Now if memory is the place where the past can yield its truths and be healed, then the Jews are right not to let go. They are right not to forgive or forget.

This is severe and, to tender-hearted Christianity, frightening. But the tender-heartedness of official Christianity is sometimes sentimental rather than realistic. Forgiveness, which is the heart of the Christian gospel, is a real struggle. It cannot be imposed or required, In fact it only works if it is both voluntary and very precisely focused. Generalised waffle about forgiveness prolongs the insult because it refuses to acknowledge real anger or conflict. Today we are drifting further and further away from Christianity. Our problem is not that people find it difficult to forgive, rather that people refuse to forgive. And this, not for serious moral and religious reasons, as with the Jews, but more because holding on to injury has become a matter of self-esteem. Victims of past outrages are wheeled out for the cameras year after year to express their unyielding hatred of those who have wronged them, and to wish them an eternity in hell. So when is it right to forgive, and why did Jesus urge us to do so? The challenge of forgiveness is that it requires a moral change, not only in the aggressor, but in the victim. The victim is not under any obvious moral requirement to exercise forgiveness; it is a decision they must make which will stretch them *beyond* what could reasonably be expected. Yet the Christian Gospel is unequivocal in urging the victim to must make this terrible effort. Why? I believe the answer has something to do with the importance of time; that time is the place of creativity and new life, and time must move on. Such movement is possible either when the aggressor recongnises what he or she has done, and asks for forgiveness, or when the person who has been wronged is able to make an act of loving imagination towards the person who has wronged them. Such acts can be transformative.

One thinks of the late Pope John Paul II visiting his would be assassin, Mehmet Ali Acga, in his prison cell. Reconciliation was possible, but in this case it was the victim who took the moral initiative. Forgiveness is possible because it is God who holds all memory. God counts the days and the years, the times and the seasons, the birth days and the death days. Wounds cannot be healed before they are acknowledged, grievance cannot be relinquished until it is owned. This is the central message of a book by Rowan Williams – a study of the resurrection stories in the New Testament.[1] He shows how the early preaching of the Church was rooted in the healing of memories. Peter and Paul and Stephen preached to the people of Jerusalem, to those who had judged and condemned Jesus. The hearers were, in the words of the King James Bible, 'cut to the heart'. They heard the gospel as accusation. Yet the provocation was not given to destroy, but to heal. At the heart of the apostles' message was the surprise: the crucified is risen.

---

[1] *Resurrection*, Darton, Longman and Todd, 1982.

The crucified returns, not to condemn but to speak peace, and not only to his friends, but to his enemies and judges.

I believe that those who burn with painful memories are waiting for that movement in which the aggressor turns to them as victim and seeks mercy from them. Their own freedom and transformation depend on the guilty coming to them with the gift of true acknowledgement, true contrition. In the case of relations between Christians and Jews the Jewish community does not find Christians capable of truly owning their guilty past. So the future remains divided, polite, diplomatic; like many broken marriages.

Rowan Williams suggests in his study of the resurrection narratives that the *personal* quality of the accounts is crucial for our understanding. Peter and Thomas and Mary and the travellers to Emmaus were friends of Jesus. They meet the risen one near to the place where they lost him. Not in the precise place, but a little way on. For all of them there is a journey. Mary goes to the garden and seeks her lost love among the tombs. Peter meets the Lord by the lakeside in the place where he first heard the call to follow. Now the call is renewed, from the other side of betrayal. The charcoal fire burns in the cold sunrise as it did on the early morning of Jesus' condemnation.

These stories ring true. The grieving and the guilty know there is a search to be made. There is a returning again and again to the place of original promise. But supposing there can be no such reconciliation? Supposing the aggressor continues to refuse to acknowledge that they have done. I believe that forgiveness can, must, still be offered, but this time, as an act of defiance, a simple refusal to let evil have the last word; a risky bid for freedom in a world otherwise dominated by the lust for revenge. It is this kind of defiance Nelson Mandela practised in his years of captivity, refusing to let himself be brutalized by the attitudes of his captors, resisting their attempt to turn him into the mirror image of themselves. Such courage, such refusal to be destroyed by hatred generates the moral energy which can genuinely unlock the past.

It is God who gives us back our memories, who hides our secrets in his heart. Sadness and loss, bereavement and guilt, defiance and resolution beat their long rhythms in our heads and hearts, driving us back to God.

The wisdom of the sun and the wisdom of the night

God gives us back our memories with accuracy and tenderness. As a sign and agent of the redemption of time God gives us his child Jesus to be our victim. All the rage and hate of the human heart and brain, known and unknown, concealed and unconcealed are exposed in the crucifixion and brought to healing in the resurrection.

Jesus is the wisdom and the Word of God, the true image of the Father. We need that wisdom, the wisdom of the light. Jesus is the great golden sun who crosses the horizons of our time, bringing illumination. He makes conscious to us all that we are and have been. He restores us to ourselves. He is our revealer and our revelation. The wisdom of Jesus comes to us through conscious 'following', through the choices that we make, through acts of kindness, study, prayer.

But there is another wisdom that we need if we are to be healed in time. We need not only the wisdom of the sun, but the wisdom of the night. We need not only the wisdom of the brain; logic and practicality, reason and commonsense, knowledge and discernment. We need also the wisdom of the body; the wisdom of desire, revulsion, awe and horror, beauty and fascination. When the Church ignores or denigrates such things its faith in the Creator dies. For the Lord made the flesh with its own wisdom and its pain, to teach us that we are dust and not God.

It was obvious to the early Christian fathers that God revealed himself not only through Jesus, the Word, but also through the Spirit of prophecy and vision. The modern Church, however, has kept the two aspects of Christian wholeness far apart from each other. Theologians are rarely visionaries; those who have mystical experience keep it hidden from the sceptical eye of the theologians. And neither group has really come to terms with the shocking fact of 'the Word made flesh'. The wisdom of the night, of the body and blood, of the feminine, is not properly integrated into the life and doctrine of the Christian Church. It exists, but in a split-off state, causing reactions that border on the fanatical.

The apparitions of Medjugorje

I began to realize this many years ago when I was involved in a
series of films about apparitions of the Virgin Mary. My
Catholic friends, most of them solidly liberal post-Vatican II
Catholics, found my interest in these phenomena baffling. But
I found they deepened my understanding, not only of Roman
Catholicism, but of the way religion needs to address the dark
side of human memory. In 1986, before the break up of
Yugoslavia, I made a film about the long-running series of
apparitions of the Blessed Virgin Mary in Medjugorje. These
apparitions and prophecies are still arousing interest over a
quarter of a century since they began. They attract large
numbers of pilgrims from all over the world. I found the
visionaries of Medjugorje to be ordinary young people,
members of a relatively poor farming community. The messages they claimed to be receiving set huge challenges for the
Church and for the nations. The Blessed Virgin spoke through
them about future chastisements which would fall upon the
earth. She urged them to prayer and repentance. She warned
them against materialism and disbelief. She wept with them
and begged them to pray for peace.

The visionaries also explained that the Church and the
world are under trial. Christians are being tested in a hundred
years of temptation, rather as Job was tested by Satan. There
are two particular pressure points on the Christian Church.
One affects marriage and the other the priesthood.

I was moved and impressed by Medjugorje. I found it
impossible to believe that the visionaries were lying or that
they were mentally deluded. The main points of their message
seemed to me to be true. Our world *is* living through dangerous times. The Church *is* tried and tested by modernity.
There *are* enormous questions about marriage and priesthood.

I found that Medjugorje was a place that I could pray in.
One day I took a photograph which had been precious to me
in my marriage and left it on the mountainside near to the
place where the first apparition occurred. I sat for a while and
watched the morning moon hang in the sky above the stone
cross on the opposite mountain. I felt nothing. But afterwards
there was a lightening of my spirits. It was as though I had left
what was broken and dead to the ultimate source of rest and
healing. It was no longer *my* burden. The past of my marriage

belonged to God. The secrets of our hearts were enfolded in God's memory, in the maternal holding of God, who is mother as well as father. This was the beginning of a process of genuine 'letting go' which came at the end of pain and not as a substitute for it. I no longer needed to be conscious of injury all the time.

Yet I remain agnostic about whether it is the Virgin Mary who inspired the visionaries. I simply do not know what it would mean to say that she appeared to them. For Mary, even more than Jesus, is not only a historical person but a focus for Christian imagination. What the visionaries reported is the Mary of popular piety; the Mary of the Rosary, of Lourdes and Bernadette. How could it be otherwise?

In spite of my agnosticism this strong feminine apparition is still experienced as a prophetic and healing force which seems to emerge from the pressures that beat on our world, or to arise from the heart of its pain. It does not seem remarkable to me that in an over-masculine world the female spirit should manifest itself in these terms. Or that in a church which has tended to think of God in almost exclusively male terms a strong female image should not rise up as the mother of sorrows.

But what is not always recognised is the ambiguity of visionary experience. Because it is suspect to the Church it remains primitive; it comes from the place where the divine and the demonic are not so easily distinguished. Perhaps that is why the Blessed Virgin of Medjugorje is always warning of the presence of Satan. Satan *is* close, as fear and darkness, terror and destructiveness. There is a punitive, judgemental side to the messages that come through the visionaries. This is not easy to interpret. The people of Medjugorje certainly felt persecuted when I visited them; there was palpable tension between the Catholic Croats and the Orthodox Serbs. We had a Serb 'minder' on our filming trip, who was treated with barely disguised contempt by the villagers. They certainly felt the Serbs were against them and resented government policy in almost every walk of life. But being governed by people they regarded as enemies also provided them with a con-venient excuse to put all the darkness outside themselves, and not to explore the possibility of evil within.

While I was staying near the village my assistant producer

was leafing through a history book when he discovered that
the region around Medjugorje was the setting for some of the
most horrific crimes of the last war. Just two miles from the
place of the first apparition, almost exactly forty years before it
took place, the Catholic Croatians did to death several hundred Serbian women and children. The victims were marched
up a mountain and thrown down on to vicious rocks. I was
astonished to discover this, and asked various members of the
community to tell me more about it. But this was the no-go
area, the area of shame and silence. The appearance of the
Blessed Virgin seemed to have had no effect on that terrible
memory. Some of the priests were prepared to admit the truth
of what had happened but did not see the apparitions as having
any connection with the wartime past. There were certainly
no very obvious signs of reparation on the part of the
Catholics, though some members of the Serbian community
showed interest in the revelations. The unwillingness of the
community to acknowledge the past baffled me. I couldn't
help feeling that the appearance of a weeping madonna so near
to the scene of the butchery might have a meaning that had so
far eluded the recipients of the revelation. But who was I to
tell? Like Joseph's dreams the visions may have a twist in them
that has not yet been recognised. There is an incompleteness
about the phenomenon, as though the times are yet to be
fulfilled.

The tragic thing is that the insights of Medjugorje are not
truly accessible to the Church's daytime wisdom; nor is the
Church's theology grounded in the passion and anxiety of the
night season. The two are separate; so that from the beginning
the Medjugorje enthusiasts have tended to become moralistic
and judgemental, while their critics have seen nothing of value
in either the apparitions or the messages.

Mother and child

In the iconography of the Church the Blessed Mother and the
Son of God belong together. Mary brings Jesus from
the womb's night into daylight. She also cradles in her arms the
body of the crucified Lord. The sun of righteousness arises into
consciousness through the Christmas stories. But the sun also
sinks in death beyond the horizons of our desire and despair.

Jesus, God's Son and the sun of the heavens, dies on the cross. He dies to the light and there is darkness over the earth. Faith portrays Jesus, crucified and dead, held in the arms of his mother. This is the mother of sorrows, and she is known by all who grieve. She is strong, she is broken, she is steadfast, she mourns:

> Lady of silences
> Calm and distressed
> Torn and most whole
> Rose of memory
> Rose of forgetfulness
> Exhausted and life-giving
> Worried reposeful
> The single Rose
> Is now the Garden
> Where all loves end...[2]

The picture of Jesus and his mother is a healing image. It leaves our memories open to change. While love waits, the universe can be reconstellated. Matter and spirit are vulnerable to the possibility of resurrection. Love, in this context, is maternal. It can do nothing but be itself. It cannot reverse death. It cannot enact justice. It can only keep vigil, *holding* what is broken and dying or dead.

The wisdom of the night is a wisdom that comes with exhaustion and anxiety. Night is full of shadows and fear because we cannot see our way and our power to act is reduced. Yet night allows the body and the mind to rest. It gives us permission to be tired and helpless in sleep. In sleep we are held by the unsleeping Lord. God does not die in the night. As a sign of presence he gives us moonlight and starlight. We cannot see our way from them but we know that our times are counted. God holds us in love, with all our memories, conscious and unconscious. Out of our memories, held and faced and let go of, God allows us to create with him the meaning of our lives. There is night and day. There are times and seasons. Also as a sign he gives us the healing image of Mary. It is Mary who gives God his birth in time; she is the

---

[2] From T. S. Eliot, 'Ash Wednesday'.

mother of God. Mary is historical and beyond history. She belongs to the outer and the inner universe. She is known to Christian devotion as the star of the sea, and she is imaged by the moon.

Summary

On the fourth day God creates the stars. These provide us with a cosmic calendar. The implication of the text is that God honours history. Time and change are spiritually important, and biblical religion offers no escape from time.

In parallel with our discovery of the outer universe is the process of making an inner world of meanings. Our earliest experiences lay down the pattern of meanings which will determine our life. We reflect on the story of Joseph as an example of God's progressive self-revelation on the course of one personal history.

Time is where we are wounded and where we can be healed, through memory. We look at the implications of this for understanding forgiveness.

To grow into maturity through prayer we need two kinds of wisdom, the daytime wisdom of reason, and the night-time wisdom of the unconscious. We consider the apparitions of Medjugorje and the role of Mary in symbolising the wisdom of the night. The challenge to us is to differentiate the two wisdoms and then to integrate them.

Suggestions for prayer

1 Say the word 'remember' over and over again to yourself. Then write down the first ten things that come into your mind. Ask the Spirit of God to show you why you need to remember these things, and what they mean to you.
2 Using a photograph album choose three pictures from the past which have particular meaning for you today. Tell God why they are important to you. Try to realise that their significance to you makes them significant for God.
3 Recall the next important anniversary of the year. Reflect on the feelings it evokes in you, of joy or sadness, or a mixture, or nothing. Bring the feelings and thoughts to God.

4 Think of a person whose forgiveness you need. In the presence of God, imagine that they are present with you. What happens if you ask them for forgiveness?

5 Think of a person who needs your forgiveness. In the presence of God imagine that they are present with you. What happens when they ask you for forgiveness?

6 Look at the night sky. The universe is far bigger than the authors of Genesis could have imagined. Where, now, do you imagine God to be? Make your answer the basis of a time of wordless prayer.

7 Revisit a powerful dream or a strong emotional experience in which you have sensed the presence or guidance of God. In your prayers ask God to deepen your intuition and open your experience to the wisdom of his Word and Spirit.

Day Five

Monsters of the Deep

*And God said, 'Let the waters bring forth swarms of living crea-
tures, and let birds fly above the earth across the dome of the sky.'
So God created the great sea monsters and every living creature that
moves, of every kind, with which the waters swarm, and every
winged bird of every kind. And God saw that it was good. God
blessed them, saying, 'Be fruitful and multiply and fill the waters
in the seas, and let birds multiply on the earth.' And there was
evening and there was morning, the fifth day.* (Gen. 1:20–23)

On the fifth day of creation God makes things that swarm in
the waters and wing across the skies. His interest is in living
creatures that move and breed with the air currents and the
sea-tides.

The primeval swarm
First in order of creation are the sea monsters. We may think
of whales and sharks, but the writers of the account were no
doubt also thinking of the mythical sea dragon, Leviathan who
is mentioned in the Psalms and the Book of Job We might
think of our own legendary creatures from the deep. There is
the Loch Ness monster. There are the killers of the sea of
fiction and film, Moby Dick and Jaws.

There are two things that people normally do with dragons
and mythical monsters. One is to fight them. The other is to
pretend they do not exist. Perhaps the removal of St George
the dragon-slayer from the Church's calendar of saints marks a
transition from the aggressive strategy to the dismissive one!
The writers of Genesis are neither aggressive nor dismissive
about the creatures that move through the seaways and

airways. They are the first living creatures who reproduce sexually, and in this respect they are especially blessed by God. They are commanded to multiply and fill the sea and the earth.

If we look at this passage from our human point of view we can see that the swarms of sea and air occupy space that we are not at home in. They live above and below us. They are not quite in human space, but they impinge on it. Human beings are bounded on either side by beasts stranger, higher, deeper than themselves. These creatures move freely and flexibly in the currents of God's sea-tides and air-streams.

If we look at the rest of the Bible we can see that God enjoys his wild creatures, especially the monsters: 'There go the ships, and Leviathan that you formed to sport in it' (Ps. 104:26). God seems to take a special delight in the great, clumsy, scaled or plated, finned or feathered creatures. He plays with them. They have peculiar significance for God. When God confronts Job 'out of the whirlwind' it is to point out not the solution to the problem of human suffering, but the mysterious splendour of the crocodile. Why?[1]

We have to remember that the priestly account of the creation with which we are concerned carries dark undertones of a more ancient civilisation. The writers of Genesis knew of other epics describing creation. In the Babylonian saga Marduk, the king of gods, pierces and slays Tiamat, the chaos monster of the sea. From her broken body the worlds and the stars are made. Echoes of this primeval myth are found all over the Old Testament, and there are here, in a disguised form, at the beginning of the book called Genesis, 'Origins'. The 'waste and void' which precede creation, the watery chaos over which the Spirit of God broods, is called in Hebrew *tohuwabohu*. The words *sound* like resounding confusion, darkness and danger.

There is no primeval battle in the Old Testament account. God is greater than Marduk. The divine authority does not need to be established by conflict. The world is made from nothing, or, more precisely, from the action of God's breath and word on the *tohuwabohu*, which is the nearest the Hebrews can get to the idea of nothing. As for the cosmic dragon who

[1] See Job 41.

wrestled with the king of gods in the pagan account, she is demoted, secularised and made multiform. She has no obvious connection with the watery chaos but slips into creation on the fifth day along with whales, sharks, crocodiles, birds and fish. Instead of being God's opponent, she is God's creature.

And yet from other parts of the Bible we can see that the sea monsters are never quite safe. God plays with them, but nowhere is there any idea that it is all right for us to. Jonah is swallowed by a whale and rescued by God's intervention. Inside the whale he confronts his own guilt and inner darkness, and then is spewed back into the world. In other places Leviathan is a name which summons up memories of the power of Egypt, Israel's traditional foe.

Even in the Bible the monsters stand for more than reptiles, sea mammals and fish. They are seen to be dark and swarming things, and feared. We retain the primitive fear of the swarm, whether they be birds, sharks or killer bees. They stand for *things* that are wild, things that are primitive, things that reproduce themselves sexually, as we do, but are in other respects so different from us.

Writers and film-makers know about our terror of creatures that are driven by instinct, without separate faces. Think of Alfred Hitchcock's film of Daphne du Maurier's terror story, *The Birds*. There was one magnificent shot in which a single feathered creature was seen in close-up, looking down on the destruction to come. This was the bird of cold animal judgement, the bird that observes without recognition, the pitiless angel of doom. When I saw the film *Jaws* on television I was held against my will. I had other things to do, but I could not switch off. The drama of the mindless destroyer, pitted against humankind, compelled me as it has millions of others. The most terrifying scene in *Jurassic Park* was when the winged raptors ran amok inside the human laboratory which was responsible for re-creating them. We are spellbound by such tales because they dramatise the conflict of our frail human intelligence and cunning with the unconscious forces of the deep.

I remember as a child being taken to the Natural History Museum in South Kensington and being astonished at the looming skeleton of the dinosaur Diplodocus in its cathedral-like setting. It seemed as improbable that such a beast once walked on earth as that babies came from their mothers' tummies.

Yet palaeontology can show us remains of such creatures and demonstrate that reptiles of the sea and the land and bony flying things did once hold dominion over the planet. They were not intelligent, but they were strong and well-adapted to life on earth. They disappeared mysteriously, leaving the way clear for the development of mammal life. So we know, through the history of the earth as well as through the Bible, that reptilian monsters are more primitive than we are. They are not intelligent, they are cold and instinctive.

What the monsters mean
The knowledge of these beasts gives shape to the primitive layers of our own personalities. They belong to older and deeper strata of existence. And so they carry mythological significance for us. We want to understand them with our minds, because it is with our minds that we demonstrate our superiority. Fantasy and science fiction allow us to do this. The fundamentalists believe that human beings and dinosaurs lived together on earth. The desire to comprehend the existence of real monsters, to wrestle with them and gain mastery is strong in us.

For the Genesis account is not only a celebration of birds and fish and sea mammals and reptiles. When those creatures appear they appear also as symbols. We are talking about what the creatures of the sea and air represent to the human imagination. The swarms and the sea monsters are reflected in our own depths. Like a medieval bestiary the creatures of Genesis are as much about the stormy contents of our inward seeing as they are about the creatures in the zoo and museum. Perhaps more so.

So how do we pray with the creatures of the deep and of the winds? One thing that seems obvious is that if we are to pray at all for any length of time we shall find at some stage that the deep is stirred, the air above us rustles and the monsters and the flying things come to life within us and around us.

This is to talk in pictures. Yet what I mean is that prayer opens us to psychic and emotional conflict. It stirs primitive memories, fears, desires and passions. Often these are formless

and worldless. They come from times before we had words to
describe our longing and pain. They manifest, sometimes as
bodily discomfort, sometimes as distraction or boredom,
sometimes as oppressive thoughts or vague feelings of dread
and fear.

At another level we might find ourselves dreaming of flight
or pursuit, of blind bats hitting us with wings or scaly things
pressing up from the floor. Birds appear, trapped and feathery,
or baby birds smashed to the ground. Giant eggs crack and
monsters ooze out.

I remember a particularly vivid dream when I was slightly
fevered after an injection against cholera and typhoid. I had a
small basil plant growing on my window-sill at the time. In
the dream I came towards the sill, and as I did so one of the
leaves of the basil plant was transformed into the hood of a
king cobra. The snake reared up out of the plant and hissed at
me with a flickering tongue! A Greek scholar would know
that the dream contained a pun for 'basil' is the Greek word
for king. The dream was terrifying in its power to shock. I
wondered afterwards at the brain's ability to scramble
experience and replay it in striking and universal images.

I believe that the monsters of the deep, the things that swarm
and fly, exist in the human mind as representations of
instinctive drives and forces. These include the body's will to
survive, which may be independent of my conscious desire;
they also include that in me which could kill in rage or under
threat. It includes the animal aspects of fear and the animal need
for comfort and closeness. It includes the instinct towards sex
and true hunger. These drives influence my conscious life all
the time. Sometimes I am aware of them and sometimes I am
not. But there are always aspects of which I am unaware, which
go deep and which stir themselves up from time to time.

Freud developed the idea of the unconscious as a layer of
the personality where unacceptable material lies repressed.
Much of it, he believed, was sexual memory from infancy and
childhood.

Jung speaks of 'the shadow' which he saw as the less-
developed, more primitive aspect of the self. Personal growth,
for him, meant acknowledging the shadow and discovering
how to incorporate the creative aspects of it into conscious
life. Spiritual writers now also talk about encounters with the

dark side of the self. There is no progress in prayer, or perhaps not even a true beginning without some encounter with the unconscious.

Baptism – an immersion in the deep

Christian life begins with baptism. In the original imagery of baptism there is a real going down into the water, an immersion in forces that are both destructive and cleansing. I once saw a film of a baptism ceremony performed by one of Kenya's independent churches on the shores of the Indian ocean. The candidate, the officiants and most of the congregation waded in among the rollers. Then the candidate was held right under a giant wave. Everyone was shouting and laughing and getting wet. But it was a serious business. Those waves could be killers. There was no mistaking the power of the sea.

The new life of Christ requires a death, death to old habits and sins and ingrained ways. Baptism includes exorcism. The false powers that possess me and drive me are cast out, sent to the place they belong. Baptism means death, to the tyranny of the false self which has been nurtured by the powers and seductions of this world. All these deaths and the hopes that go with them are spelt out in the baptismal promises.

The liturgy of baptism speaks of a rebirth, a return to innocence. What is washed away is the guilt that accrues to primal sin, the inheritance of shame and falsehood.

The difficulty, in Christian experience, is in identifying what it is that has to be died to, and what it is to come to rebirth. When I think of the rollers of the Indian ocean, the green sunlit sea and the white foam, it seems that baptism signifies an immersion in life *and* death, and they are not opposed to each other, but somehow intertwined. I put my life in danger. I expose what I know of myself to the fierce waves and the torrent beneath the waves. I go down into the depths to rediscover my primal self, which is both animal and spiritual. And that is where I find Christ, the Word made flesh. Baptism should make me more human, more alive, more accepting of the ambivalences within myself. It should give me courage to accept the dark and the unknown and to learn from my body and my own instinctive drives.

Some years ago I went to church in an area I did not know
to find there was to be a baptism in the middle of the service.
The candidates were a little girl of seven and her baby brother.
The young priest who officiated took the opportunity to
preach a sermon. Most of it was directed at the seven-year-old.
From now on, the young man said, you have a special
responsibility to *be good*. Jesus is watching over you, and if you
are naughty it will make him very sad. So it's up to you to be
kind and helpful to your parents, not to be selfish, to think of
others, to work hard at school, to obey your father and help
mummy with the housework.

This was the burden that came with that child's baptism, the
price she was expected to pay for the privilege of being named
an acceptable member of the Christian community. I felt a
grief for that child, and also for the Church which is so capable
of distorting the gospel of God. For if that child carries out the
priest's instructions she will begin a long process of denying
her true self and operating out of a false, idealised self. She will
learn to smile and control her anger and joy. She will learn not
to react to her own wants and needs but always to comply
with what others expect of her. She will be socialised into
Christian womanhood as millions have been before her.

And this is what has often happened in Christian experience. The new life of Christ has been presented as a life where
the will subdues and dominates the instincts. It is seen as a life
of control over the inner darkness. Instead of going down into
the waters of death and coming up alive, with the primal
instincts re-energised because accepted, baptism signifies a
death to the life of the body and a cold aridity in which life is
directed by the intellect and the will. Instead of being seen as a
source of grace, the instincts and the body are identified with
the dragon, with evil and danger. Christian coldness rules by
denial and repression and masks its true nature in the rhetoric
of freedom and love. Instead of being incorporated into Christ
the Christian self incorporates the monster into conscious life
and becomes cold, cut off, depressed, un-alive.

The denial of the monsters
I feel strongly about this because I have lived most of my adult
life within the Christian Church, and I have worked with

Christians in a variety of different contexts. And, of course, I am a Christian myself. I am constantly depressed by the lying that we indulge in, by the denial of anger and pain, by the guilt and the secrecy that operate in church-based groups. Why has this happened?

Through the centuries the Church has waged war on the body and the unconscious. It has carried the war outside itself and projected its hatred of the instincts on to women, non-Christians, Jews, foreigners – anyone who could be seen as 'different'.

Many have patiently carried the burden of darkness that good Christians have preferred not to acknowledge within themselves. Those who have had the courage to see the dark ambivalences within have sometimes been pressed to fight them down. There are numerous examples of well-meaning Christians torturing themselves with absurd and exaggerated disciplines in an attempt to control what is wild and primitive within.

Today's Church is more likely to deny or domesticate the monsters. We have been taught, like the newly-christened little girl, to belong to 'the nice and the good'.

But it is always the case that those who deny the dragon are the ones who are most in danger of being swallowed up by it. As an Anglican I know the Church of England best. The Church of England that I grew up in was a gentlemanly, well-meaning Church. In my adult life I recognize the fruits of this. It was a Church of intellectual freedom and disciplined study, a Church for gentle eccentrics and wild depressives who were somehow contained by its blandness. I loved the cool formality of cathedral evensong. I could cope with low church enthusiasm and relished high church ceremonial. It was a Church which denied the dragon within. This meant that it functioned, but with low energy. Depression was frequent among the clergy. But now the mood in society is much more strident and confrontational. The different 'parties' of the Church seem all too ready to regard their opponents as barely Christian, and certainly not as 'genuine' Anglicans. When there is a public row it erupts with all the violence of a monster breaking out of chains. Think of the venom unleashed on women, homosexuals, and the occasional unorthodox bishop, by various fighting sections of this once quiet, rather dull, respectable church. The public message about Anglicanism in general and the Church of England in particular is that it is an unruly house, always at war with itself. We see again and again not penitence, humility and charity, but self-righteousness and aggression. Watching the decline in public reticence and good manners within the Church has been one of the most heartbreaking aspects of my life as a priest. Now the monsters are out and who knows where they will take us?

The beauty of the beast

The tragedy is that by denying the great monsters while they were accessible within ourselves we cut ourselves off not only from truth but from primitive vitality, power and beauty. Now the monsters are out they can do us no good at all, they are beyond control. We see them in the 'enemy' because we have denied them in ourselves. Yet in the Bible God boasts of his monsters. He delights in them and plays with them. The God of the Psalms is one who himself travels on the wings of the wind. His storm clouds raise the tempest over the deep. There are times when God invites us to ride the dragon, to make fire, to walk on the water.

We need to remember that it is not only our niceness that God has created but our wildness as well. The problem is putting them together so that they stop making war on one another. Colin Morris, who was a Methodist missionary in Africa, described a fellow missionary who impressed him deeply. This man took a secret delight in creeping up on lions and staring into their eyes. Perhaps that helped him to see the wildness in himself, the wildness without which he could never be whole or true before God.

The God of the Bible is quite unscrupulous. He will use our wildness for his own ends: 'Human wrath serves only to praise you' (Ps. 76:10). He used Elijah's fury, Jeremiah's depression and Ezekiel's madness. Having used our savagery for his own inscrutable purposes he will then reveal it to us mercilessly in order to help us to wholeness. So we are equipped with the gospel of peace, which is not a strategy for repressing wildness, but a way of living with and learning from the dark energies.

Two examples from the Bible. First Elijah. Elijah is seen as the prophet of prophets, a legendary wild man who carried the word of the Lord against a deceiving king and queen of Israel. He saw the darkness of false worship engulfing Israel and he challenged the priests of the alternative faith to a bizarre contest. Winning the battle with God's help he butchered his opponents. Now he was a marked man, marked by his violence without and within. Eventually rage drove him into the heart of the wilderness. There God confronted him with terrifying signs which revealed the violent fantasies of his own heart. Yet God was not in the earthquake, wind or fire. Eventually, when the fantasies faded God was there in 'a sound of sheer silence'. Then, when Elijah was at last able to 'hear' the silence, he hid his face and stood before God, ready now to respond to him from a place of truth and not fantasy (I Kings 19:11-14).

If Elijah was the greatest of the prophets, Moses was the giver of the law. But the biblical narrative presents us with a Moses who is a guilt-ridden coward, hiding from his past. God called him to confront the king of Egypt with his people's claims to freedom. Moses was full of self-doubt. He knew that he did not ring true, and that even his voice betrayed him, for he had a stammer. He had a secret crime on his heart, the murder of an Egyptian foreman. He knew that he could not speak for God, 'suppose they do not believe me or listen to me' (Exod. 4:1).

Yet God knew about his crime, and the inner wildness which Moses was hiding from him. God commanded Moses to cast his rod upon the ground. The rod became a snake. And snakes, as we know, are related to monsters. They are the wingless dragons of the earth. Moses was commanded to catch the snake by the tail. It was a dangerous strategy, but he managed it. In his hand the snake turned back into a rod.[2]

Through this encounter Moses was able to get in touch with his own wildness. Yet this time it did not overcome him. The wildness remained in the rod. He had access to its energy and vitality without being destroyed by it.

But it is not so easy. It is sometimes assumed that if only

---

[2] The nature of the rod is something of a mystery. One strand of the narrative uses a word which suggests a shepherd's staff, another describes it as 'the rod of God', a kind of supernatural wand.

Christians have faith and hope for the best tragedy and negativity can be avoided. There is an easy-going Christian optimism which teaches that even the worst of our inner monsters can be transformed into blessings. But this is not always so. Shadows that come into the light cease to be shadows. They disappear. Or at least, they have a tendency to *re*-appear, firmly attached to someone else. Perhaps to some poor unfortunate who 'has problems recognising the shadow side of himself'!

I have myself sometimes assumed that the work of growth in Christ was to make conscious and visible all that was dark and shadowy within. Sometimes I think there is truth in this, and there are hidden aspects of ourselves which we need to befriend and make conscious if we are to grow to wholeness.

I once gave a talk at a retreat about making friends with the monsters and dragons of the deep. I outlined the dangers of denying or fighting them and then ended with a meditation on Jesus in the wilderness, where, according to Mark 1:13, he was 'with' the wild beasts. I said that I found the word 'with' very significant. For the Lord did not dominate the beasts or deny them. He was simply able to be with them, at peace. I recommended my retreatants to 'make friends with their dragons'! Later we all assembled for Evensong. To my horror one of the appointed psalms was Psalm 74 which recalls the myth of the cosmic battle over the waters: 'You divided the sea by your might; you broke the heads of the dragons in the waters. You crushed the heads of Leviathan' (vv. 13–14).

My first thought was that it was an appalling trick for God to work through the compilers of the lectionary to embarrass me in such a way. But it set me thinking. I found myself reflecting on the ambivalence towards the sea monsters which the Bible shows.

Shadows are shadows, and dragons are not domestic beasts. They live underground, beneath the sea, in a pagan half-lit world, and that is where they need to be if they are to help us and warn us.

Even God, it seems, doesn't always play with Leviathan. The important thing seems to be that the monsters know their place. If they get too important, or start having pretensions to dominate, then God lashes out at them. The waters are divided. The worlds are made. Israel crosses into freedom. God uses the dark energies creatively, to make something new.

The snake and the font

All this requires a depth of discernment and study and experience which is not easy to find in the world or the Church. We are not at ease with ambivalence, and most of us have not spent the time in the desert which would enable us to make true distinctions between good and evil. Our notions of good and evil are too simple and too separate. Because of this our Christian life has lost its energy and our prayers are empty and passionless. And yet there is an ancient, primal wisdom waiting to be discovered, to be quarried from the Church's memory, and from our own.

A few years before I left the world of television I spent a night in Istanbul on the way to make a film in the ancient city of Ephesus. On the first evening I visited the magnificent blue mosque which overlooks the sea on the west side of the city. The next morning I went back to visit the church of the Holy Wisdom, which stands a stone's throw from the mosque. The great basilica was built by the emperor Justinian in 537 and dominated eastern Christendom for nine centuries. I imagined the ships of the Byzantine empire sailing home from the sea of Marmara to harbour round the Golden Horn. The sailors would clearly see the dome of the immense church, and they would know that inside the mosaics on the vault represented the heavens and all the stars.

In the fifteenth century the conquering Turks turned the church into a mosque. Now it is little more than a museum. When I saw it the great mosaics were obscured by scaffolding, and the dome was dusty and neglected. But as I came out, rather disappointed, I saw in the vestibule a wide and open stone font. I could not tell how old it was, but round its open rim a huge stone serpent was coiled, with its tail dipping down towards the water. Because it was so unexpected I felt quite startled. The font was dry and unused but the warning snake remained.

It has seemed to me since to be almost a symbol for what many encounter in the Christian Church today. The sources of wisdom are dried up, the waters of healing no longer flow. Yet the great snake remains, guarding the site with moral prohibitions and dogmatic pronouncements. We know there should be life there, we know that there once was, and could be again, but all we see is the snake.

The irony is that the Church does not yet have any notion of its own deadness. It sees itself as a caring, loving and righteous body when it is often experienced as untruthful, unalive, lacking both intellectual energy and compassion. It denies the snake, and at the same time denies its access to its own wisdom.

For in some odd way the snake and the font belong together. The snake is about primal energy and danger. It is very close to evil and temptation. The serpent is subtle. Part of its subtlety is that it sheds its skin. It lives through dying, through casting off what it no longer needs. So the snake becomes a symbol of immortality. The font, on the other hand, carries the symbols of cleansing, purifying and healing. But it must not be forgotten that water also drowns and destroys. Water is an element of death as well as life, and birth is a dangerous journey as well as a glad arrival.

I heard of a dream which illustrated the healing power of snakes. A woman was ill with a high fever in a country region near Atlanta in the United States. It was an area where big snakes were frequently encountered. In her dream she was asleep, and she knew that the sleep was making her better. Yet she was able to see herself, and she saw that she was lying enfolded in the coils of a giant winged boa-constrictor. The creature's feathers made a soft bed for her body, and the steady coolness of the snake's skin soothed the burning and shivering of the fever. At the end of her sleep she got up and walked away to safety.

What I am trying to say is that the symbols of the snake and the font point in two directions, towards death and life. Choosing between them is not just a matter of controlled conscious choice. It is a growth of the whole person, in which what points to life at one time may be death-bringing at another. The snake *can* be the embodiment of evil. It can take the form of the great dragon which is cast down by Michael the archangel. But Moses lifts the serpent in the wilderness and it pre-figures the healing wisdom of the cross.

There are times for an aggressive strategy towards the monsters of the deep, and times when they must be listened to because we need their power and healing energy. The worst strategy is to pretend they are not there.

St Teresa in *The Interior Castle* describes the courtyard of the soul as being full of little reptiles worrying away, biting and scratching. Her advice is to recognise them and then ignore them. The task of prayer can be carried on whether they are there or not. She certainly does not suggest that you waste energy trying to remove them.

When Michael casts down the great dragon he puts him in his proper place, in the deep, in hell. He does not pretend that he doesn't exist or try to remove him from reality. The great snake too is God's creature, even when he oversteps his bounds. He is related to Leviathan. And Leviathan is still the sea dragon of Babylonian mythology, whom God plays with, though it is dangerous for us to.

One of the things that struck me when I visited the cathedral at Chartres was how the saints and prophets are depicted along with their devils. In stone and glass they stand and it is crystal clear that the demon or animal at their feet is part of their story. It lies crouched, defeated or compliant, but still *there*, still in some way essential to the holiness of the individual. The art of the lives of saints, and why their lives are important is that they learnt to distinguish between good and evil. They faced the ambiguity of their own natures and discovered what belonged where. Often their attempts to be true led them into deep suffering. They were frequently misunderstood by their fellow Christians because their sense of good and evil was rarely contained by the bounds of contemporary morality.

So there is the challenge to our praying. Can we discern our own monsters, respect them and allow them to guard us and teach us what they know? Can we bash them on the head when they need to be bashed? Can we rejoice in their energy and not be overcome by their chaos? Can we discipline their passions without becoming reptilian in our coldness?

It is important for us to ask ourselves these questions. For dragons, in all the best stories, are appointed to guard great treasures.

Summary

On the fifth day God creates the birds and sea monsters. We look at what these stand for in myth and fantasy. Then we reflect on the Bible's ambivalence to the monsters of the sea.

We reflect on the monsters as symbols of unconscious drives in the human personality. Prayer puts us in touch with these, and so do dreams. We look at baptism as a place of immersion and cleansing. We consider what is being died to in baptism and what it means to say we are reborn in Christ. I argue that Christians have sometimes repressed or denied vital and life-giving aspects of our humanity, with damaging consequences. We look at Elijah and Moses and their confrontation with dark inner forces. It is important that the dark forces are in their proper place where they can defend, warn and energise us. If they are denied or repressed they actually take over and dominate.

So the challenge to our praying is to recognise the ambivalence of what is dark and unformed within. We need to learn discernment so that we have a range of responses to what emerges from our unconscious depths.

Suggestions for prayer

1 What was your first encounter with a monster? Was it in the zoo, or in a fairy tale, or a television fantasy? Remember your feelings and thoughts. Where was God for you at the time?

2 Think of a person whom you cannot stand. Write down all the aspects of their personality that you dislike, fear or feel contempt for. What do you feel about having such feelings about another person? Are there any aspects of your own personality that you recognise in them? Make your answer the subject of a conversation with God.

3 In the prayer book of your church look up the baptismal promises. Spend some time with them, thinking about what they mean to you. What are the things you need to renounce or turn away from?

4 Fill a glass or dish with water. Spend time looking at it, feel it with your fingers or put a little on your face. Think of

the properties of water. What do they tell you about God's work in your life?

5   Read Mark 1:12–13. Spend some time in your imagination being with Jesus and the wild beasts that live in your inner desert and ask him to show you what it means to be *with* them.

6   Pinpoint an issue in your life about which you have fiercely contradictory feelings and thoughts. What could God be saying to you through the conflict? How do such conflicts usually resolve themselves in your experience? Use your answer to seek God's wisdom in your present dilemma.

7   Find a picture or an icon of St George killing the dragon, or create one in your imagination. What is the strength of the image for you? Does it give you energy or make you feel uncomfortable? Are there any circumstances in which you could imagine yourself killing? Make the answer the subject of a conversation with God.

Day Six

The Trinity and the Tragedy

And God said, 'Let the earth bring forth living creatures of every kind: cattle and creeping things and wild animals of every kind.' And it was so. God made the wild animals of the earth of every kind, and the cattle of every kind, and everything that creeps upon the ground of every kind. And God saw that it was good.

Then God said, 'Let us make humankind in our image, according to our likeness; and let them have dominion over the fish of the sea, and over the birds of the air, and over the cattle, and over all the wild animals of the earth, and over every creeping thing that creeps upon the earth.' So God created humankind in his image, in the image of God he created them; male and female he created them. God blessed them, and God said to them, 'Be fruitful and multiply, and fill the earth and subdue it; and have dominion over the fish of the sea and over the birds of the air and over every living thing that moves upon the earth.' And God said, 'See, I have given you every plant yielding seed which is upon the face of all the earth, and every tree with seed in its fruit; you shall have them for food.' And it was so. God saw everything that he had made, and indeed, it was very good. And there was evening and there was morning, the sixth day. (Gen. 1:24–31)

On the sixth day God makes land animals and human beings.

The account of creation in Genesis is sometimes criticised for being too anthropomorphic, that is, too centred on human beings. Today, when we are so conscious of the danger we humans pose to our environment, perhaps we need an account which makes us less centre-stage. Here, the creation of men and women is God's final act before he takes his rest from his work. But, according to the text, it was a quick job, taking

88

only half a day. The sea monsters and the birds took twice as long to create. We come almost as an afterthought to the domestic animals and beasts of the earth. Cats, cows, beetles and lions happened on Friday morning. We are a Friday afternoon job. Not quite finished, perhaps. And deeply dependent on the other creatures with whom we share the earth.

Yet it is possible to lose sight on our dependence. The services for use in the Church of England at the Easter Vigil offer the option of reading a drastically truncated version of the creation narrative. You can jump from verse 5 to verse 26; thus cutting out the whole of the non-human creation. What the congregation *hears* is that human beings are created immediately after the creation of light, with nothing in between!

But the Genesis account never assumes that the creation is made wholly for humankind. Men and women have their role, and it is an important one, but it is one of inter-dependence with the animal and plant creation. Our closeness to the animals is emphasised by the fact that we share the sixth day with them. We are the same sort of creatures as dogs and elephants. Like them, we require food. Like them, we reproduce sexually. The grains and seeds and leaves and roots of plants are provided for our food; and, like them, we are made twofold in order to continue. God makes us earth-bound, dependent on earth.

Image and likeness

And yet the difference between human beings and the rest of creation is a real one and needs to be affirmed. We are created in the image of God and after God's likeness, and we have a mandate from God, not only to populate the earth, but to manage it. This is a key text, and it is the basis of all biblical teaching on the nature of human beings. Men and women resemble God in some way, and have been given a task to fulfil. The resemblance, and the task, belong together. So what does the resemblance consist of? And what is the task?

Theologians down the centuries have interpreted the image and likeness of God in different ways at different times. Most have seen a closeness to God in the human capacity to reason, to transcend the natural environment by the power of thinking and the determination of the will.

Augustine said frankly that it was the human mind which was made in God's image.[1] The body, our physical desires and emotions, are therefore more distant from God and likely to lead us astray unless they are kept firmly under control. Augustine reads the text as the converted Manichee[2] that he was. It was impossible for him to see the human body, or its passions, as delightful and God-given. Nor was he alone. The vast majority of the early Christian fathers saw the desires of the body and the emotions as something rather embarrassing, and often as a hindrance to spiritual growth.

The bare text, however, does not obviously contain the meaning that the early theologians found in it. They had their reasons for what they saw, but we can see something different that involves less distortion. The text does not exactly locate the image and likeness of God for us, but it does give a strong hint of where we might look for it. It is rather a surprising one: 'Then God said, "Let us make man in our image, after our likeness"... So God created man in his own image, in the image of God he created him; male and female he created them.'

Male and female

There is a struggle of language going on here. It is a struggle between singularity and plurality in God; and a struggle between an inclusive masculine description of man and a description which allows the diversity of male and female. God, whom we usually think of as singular, is suddenly 'we'. God is consulting within his own being; God comes to a communal decision. This is odd. So is the description of 'man'. Does the word 'man' here mean male man or humanity? The Hebrew word is *adam* which is the name of the mythological first man of Chapter 2. There seems at this

---

[1] 'Not in the body, but in the mind, was man made in the image of God', Augustine, Homilies on the Gospel of John, 23.

[2] The Manichees were a sect who grew up alongside early Christianity. They believed that physical matter was deeply corrupt and spiritual freedom involved a rejection of the flesh.

point to be a recognition in the text that this is not a full description, and so it goes on to insist that the human reality be understood as twofold, male and female. Humanness, in other words, is neither exclusively male nor female. In fact it consists of the relationship between male and female.

So, man and woman together make up the image of God, who is not only 'I' but 'We'. By saying this I am not suggesting that the mind is excluded from the image, or that the early fathers were wrong to see God mirrored in our capacity to reflect on our experience. But intellectual capacity differs and changes with age and training. More basic to our identity is our gender and our search for ways to express ourselves as men and women. Part of this expression is in sexual desire and family life, part is in work and art and prayer and thinking. Men and women are not interchangeable. I cannot imagine a woman writing Augustine's *Confessions*. Nor can I see a man writing Julian of Norwich's *Revelations of Divine Love*. Both are intellectually searching and emotionally convincing. Men and women can see themselves in both. But the gender of the author does in some way colour the experience and the terms in which it is described.

The assertion that the image of God is enfolded in our sexuality has enormous implications for our understanding of the relationship between the sexes, and the importance of sexuality in our growth towards God. It suggests that the image of God is fractured when the sexes try to fulfil their task without recognising each other's humanity or when they try to dominate each other. Indeed it suggests what the God-given task actually *is* for men and women on this earth. The human vocation to 'subdue the earth' is given to man and woman in respect of the image which together they comprise. God's authority of stewardship over the earth is not given to men alone, or to women alone, but to men in partnership with women and women in collaboration with men.

We have not, however, been very successful in living out God's desire for us. We are faced with appalling problems in the management of our planet. Global warming, the growth of desert and the cutting down of the rain forest, our addiction to oil; all bear witness to a rapacious tendency to exploit and destroy our natural environment. The feminist movement analysed this disaster as one of the consequences of the male attempt to transcend nature by dominating women and exploiting the earth. The feminist critique contains an incisive biblical judgement. Through human history, aided and abetted by the institutions of religion, human males have taken unnatural authority upon themselves. They have included their female partners as part of what there is to be subdued, rather than seeing in them the necessary complementary authority to manage the planet. As a result they have brought the earth and its myriad species of plants and animals to the edge of destruction. The female aspect of the image of God has been damaged to the point where it is almost unrecognisable. Sexual isolation and violence exist alongside sexual desire and longing, and the planet suffers in consequence.

The Bible knows that this state of affairs exists, and mourns it as part of what the Christian story calls the Fall. The second narrative of creation (Gen. 3:15ff) has God's angel sundering the friendship of male and female, and driving them out into a world that has become hostile. The damage to the image of God, which is incurred by all men and women simply by being sons and daughters of Adam and Eve, is now to be set alongside the truth of our creation as equal partners.

Two pictures: (1) Rublev's icon of the Trinity

So when I read the creation account in the light of human experience I am confronted both with a promise and a dilemma. Two pictures come into my mind. One stands for the promise, one for the problem.

The first is a Russian icon, a portrayal of the Trinity (see p. xi) by the fifteenth-century artist Andrei Rublev. Rublev made the icon at a time of unrest and violence. It is an affirmation of life in the face of the chaos of war. Rublev's inspiration comes from one of the later narratives in Genesis, the story of Abraham being visited by angels.[3]

This is a strange and beautiful story. The divine travellers seek Abraham as he sits by his tent door at midday, beside the oaks of Mamre. There is something odd about the visitors. The description of them slips and slides from singular to plural, from divine to human. At the beginning of the account it is

[3] See Genesis 18.

'the Lord' who appears to Abraham. In the next verse it is 'three men'. The text says that Abraham saw 'them', but he greets them as 'My Lord'. Abraham prepares food for the stranger(s), and they ask to see Abraham's wife, Sarah. Then 'the Lord' prophesies that Sarah will have a child in the springtime. When the visitors leave they are just described as 'the men'. By the beginning of the next chapter they have become 'two angels'.

The early Christians who tried to interpret this text were fascinated by the shifts of language. To them it expressed an esoteric mystery. It was a foreshadowing of the doctrine of the Trinity. It was a revelation of a living God who does not inhabit eternal solitude but rejoices in eternal friendship. A liturgical commentary from the Orthodox tradition says, 'Blessed Abraham, thou hast seen and received the One and Triune Godhead'.

So when Rublev depicts the Trinity he shows them in the form of the three angels. In the icon you can see them, gathered around Abraham's table. One of the oaks of Mamre is in the background. The three sit round the table but they do not form a closed circle. On the table is a chalice, offered outwards. The table is an altar and the meal is a welcome, a celebration. Between the angelic figures is a flow of colour and glance, hands and folded wings, relaxation and spontaneity.

The icon seems to be showing the threefold God making himself at home among humankind. The angels come to Abraham and Sarah and the child who, though not yet physically conceived, already represents the old couple's dream of continued life and blessing. The three visitors are at home round Abraham's table. No one of the figures dominates. The figure behind the table and the figure to the right look towards the figure on the left. Is the left-hand figure God the Father, and the centre figure the Son of God? Or is it the other way round? In fact, it is the Father seated on the left, the Son behind the table and the Spirit on the right. The Son and the Spirit look to the Father but there is no sense of hierarchy. No figure is subordinated. The two look towards one, but the circle remains open. The Trinity is 'we' but its shape is one of welcome.

What is more, the figures in Rublev's icon are androgynous. The forms are not the forms of men or women, but of beings who are like men and women. They have the characteristics of both. They greet one another, and their greeting extends outwards. This is the God in whose image we are made.

Two pictures: (2) Picasso's 'The Tragedy'

The other picture which haunts me when I read about the creation of men and women is by Picasso. It is from his 'blue' period and it is called 'the Tragedy' (see p. xii). It is thought that it may have been a response to the suicide of one of his friends. The background of the picture is a blue sea, blue sand, an unnaturally heavy blue sky. Three figures dominate the three bleak strips of blue: a woman, a man and a boy. The woman is tall and straight, black-haired. She is turned away and we are impressed by her straight, proud back. She looks down. Is she cradling something in her arms? We can't see. The man stands shiftily, one leg dragging in the sand, his arms folded. His gaze too is downcast. The shape of the woman speaks to me of strength and endurance and pain. The figure of the man speaks of guilt and unspeakable need. The boy stands beside the man and looks towards the woman. One hand is stretched out to her, the other seems to be restraining the man. Is he looking at what the woman is holding in her arms? His face is full of dread, his lips slightly parted, his visible eye dull and dark with fear. There is a space between the figures, but we see only the blue.

The figures in Picasso's painting are sharply differentiated sexually. There are the man and the woman and the boy, and whatever is being held by the woman. Yet there is no communication between these figures, only a profound unease which is near to despair. Their secret is not disclosed to us. Their circle of wounded silence is complete and no one can get in. In a darker sense though, we all know the blue emptiness they occupy.

In some degree we partake of the truth of both pictures. Picasso's expresses my despair of reaching wholeness; Rublev's raises me to hope. The occupations of work, play and prayer, which comprise the human task which I have been given, require me to move from one to the other and back again, in penitence and faith, if I am to know myself, my capacities, and God.

What I have to work with is my own raw experience. The first impressions of integration and completion have come to me from my parents. At first this came almost entirely from my mother, later it came from my mother and father together. The impression of what I now seek as the image of God has been filtered into my life through them. My deepest and most primitive self-image comes from them, and it has divine and demonic dimensions. There are huge affirmations. There are tremendous gaps. Prayer happens in both extremes of experience, and between them.

Two models of the image of God

Reflecting on this suggests two rather different models of the image of God as it emerges in our experience. In one, it could be described as a dim or unfocused likeness which needs to be sharpened and developed rather like a photograph. This is a model of *development*. The image is present through the impression of the parents but needs to be realised and brought to maturity through immersion in life and the ever renewed gift of divine grace, the blessing which comes from God's deep longing for us to be free and fulfilled. Meditating on the implications of Rublev's Trinity icon may encourage the process to become conscious, and therefore communicable.

The other model starts with a broken mirror. The mirror stands for what, in me, should be capable of reflecting God's image. But the capacity has been lost. Sometimes I picture the mirror broken into two halves. This is when I am aware of elements of irreconcilable division in my primitive self-image. I cannot see God as whole when there is such damage to what reflects God to me. Sometimes I imagine the mirror as cracked and flawed. There is a complete image, but it is distorted. Sometimes, in my mind's eye, the image of God seems shattered into many pieces, some of which are lost. The task then becomes a matter of trying to reassemble the pieces of glass as far as it is possible, to catch in their edges a glimpse of the lost likeness.

Both models have their uses. We do not have to choose between them. In one sense, our creation in the image of God is a promise of natural growth and development. We receive life from our parents and a model of what it means to be human, which will affect us all life long. In another sense there is some ruin in all of us, because none of us had perfect parents, and our completion in God involves working with the damage rather than striving for an impossible ideal.

Sexuality and the image of God

Either way, the image lies within our sexuality. It is within our need to greet one another as man and woman and to be greeted. This involves recognising and owning our differences, sharing our needs and tasks and helping to complete one another physically, emotionally and spiritually. If I work with the more optimistic model, pictured for me as Rublev's icon, then love and desire are to be welcomed as paths to God. I am not complete in myself; my completion in God requires me to greet and be greeted by what is not me. That is why we love and desire, and when we fail, desire again. The second account of creation in Genesis 2 has God saying: 'It is not good for man to be alone'. The Bible assumes that the male and female are different, and it is the difference that provokes the desire of one for the other. We are not androgynous beings. The image of God is man/woman, but it is an image in which we have to grow.

Sometimes one can see this growth almost physically happening as couples over the years come to resemble each other. Often, in the second half of life, men become softer, more rounded and chubby. This is often accompanied by a greater gentleness and sensitivity. Women often become physically harder. Their features sharpen. Sometimes they become more assertive, more adventurous. It is as though some lifelong reversal is taking place, a balancing act between the sexes in which characteristics are carried for each other, mingled and transferred. A profound knowing of the other is accompanied by self-knowing.

So, the lifelong task of growing into or healing the image involves an intermingling of 'masculine' and 'feminine' attitudes and values.

The wisdom of the head and the wisdom of the heart will always make war on one another as long as they work separately. Yet they have to know themselves as separate before they can come together. The task is to know them in their different kinds of strength, and then to integrate them, as Theophan the Recluse realised in his powerful saying,: 'Put your mind in your heart and stand in the presence of God all day long.' Logical, hard-headed women, and compassionate, tenderhearted men start with an advantage. But this can also prove a threat to the world's sense of order, and they may face great difficulty, as Rosalind Franklin did (see p. 47), in being able to be themselves.

Opposites attract, and we like our opposites to be in the expected place! So heterosexual attraction, desire and fulfilment remain, for most people, the way in to human completion and growth in God. Desire is the yearning of the body for completion, the yearning of the half-self for wholeness.

But sexual life is also, for many of us, a way which passes through confusion, frustration and even betrayal. We are attracted, not only to what heals, but to what hurts. Our experience is coloured by our knowledge of tragedy. As ministers, workmates, spouses and friends we know about pain and guilt, breakdown and rejection. We know about partnerships fractured by illness and misfortune. We know about marriages destroyed by casual infidelity, sexual ignorance or indifference and violence. We know about rape. We know about the sexual abuse of children. We know about cruelty and disease within the homosexual world. We know about the persecution of homosexuals by the supposedly normal. We know about the quieter humiliations of male impotence and female frigidity.

At bleak times I have sometimes felt that the worst thing about Picasso's 'Tragedy' is that one can see echoes of a resemblance to the pattern of Rublev's 'Trinity'. Perhaps it would have been more merciful if our likeness to our Creator had been quietly rubbed out. Faced with our own and others' capacity for betrayal do we not sometimes think: 'It would have been better for that one not to have been born' (Mark 14:21)?

How can we pray our way through the blessings and contradictions of our sexual natures?

An invitation to wholeness
'Be perfect', says Jesus (Matt. 5:48), and the Greek word for
perfect, *teleios*, suggests that the Lord is inviting us to be whole,
to fulfil our destiny by completing the image of God in us as
far as we can, through God's grace. Yet Jesus does not suggest
that the flaws in the image can simply be eradicated, or that the
broken pieces can be jammed together any old how. Instead of
clobbering us over the head with ideals he invites us to share
the burden of our pain with him, to carry the cross of our
wounded nature in his company. Jesus is the model for us that
love cannot be disincarnate. Whether human or divine, love
requires a body, and the bodily experience of tenderness and
desire is a gift of our creation, given for the healing of wounds,
which issues in the renewal of life.

Marriage
This is why the Church believes in marriage, and sees stable,
permanent marriage as God's will for the majority of
humankind. For most people, falling in love with a member of
the opposite sex, forming a lifelong friendship and building a
home together is the slow, humdrum, hectic, gentle, difficult
route to maturity. Marriage gives the opportunity to develop
something of the wholeness of God's image, while fulfilling
the divine task to be fruitful and manage a part of the planet.

Marriage often seems so ordinary, so taken for granted, that
its spiritual significance for our growth in God is not always
spelt out. But in the eastern Orthodox Church young people
getting married wear crowns. The crowns have two meanings.
Man and woman stand before the altar of God playing the
parts of king and queen of creation. Vows are said which
cannot be unsaid. By their commitment to one another they
become joint priests of God's possibilities. The mingling of
bodily fluids in sexual intimacy is a sacrament of creation as
holy as the water and wine mingled at the Eucharist. Life is
being passed on through the couple, who come together
lovely, wanting, excited, vulnerable, naked as birth.

Yet the crowns have another meaning. The Church knows
that marriage is also a kind of dying that leads through martyrdom to glory. The two lovers came together to seed new
possibilities. To do this they must endure the dismantling of

defences. The end of aloneness is a willingness to die to the defended, separated self. Can the two endure this in growing trust and love? Or does the process bring anxiety, disappointment, disillusion? Marriage is either a process of dying to live, or a living death. As the couple stand before the altar praying for God's blessing, they are themselves and more than themselves. They do not know all of what they are carrying with them. The secrets and assumptions of parents and grandparents, back through the generations. The best marriages are compromises, daily dyings, in which hidden things are brought to light and patiently worked through. Yet perhaps there are very few who come through to glory, very few who win the martyr's crown. Still, the challenge is there and for most of us sex, marriage and children are the way the image of God is brought to some sort of maturity in us.

There are many 'good enough' marriages, a few glorious ones, and some sad and destructive ones which may have to be dismantled for the individuals to be saved.

So, our marriages, and the attractions that could be, or could have been, marriages; and our failures inside or outside marriage, are essential raw material for our praying. We come to God always as ourselves and more than ourselves, carrying with us, as it were, the internal image of parents, lovers and those who have healed or injured us emotionally and sexually.

Celibacy

Marriage has never been the only option for growth in God. The Church knows, in its wisdom, that the image of God is fractured in us in many different ways. Some fragments are too shattered to come close without risk of further fragmentation. For some, sexual intimacy is a real threat to what integrity the self possesses. The kind of commitment that marriage requires would deepen already existing hurts. Celibacy may seem to be the only alternative to self-destructive promiscuity. Often the choice presents itself as an experience of being chosen. The imagery of God as the divine lover plays a strong part in building the celibate's identity and self of worth.

Some opt for celibacy, not because they are personally fragile, but because they are too painfully aware of the distortions in the relationship between the sexes that run through the whole of their society. Integrity, for them, requires an essential distance from the commitments of family life. For others celibacy arise out of a hard choice between two goods, the goodness of family life and the rewards of a vocation pursued with single-mindedness. Others find themselves celibate because they have never found an appropriate partner, and find themselves eventually accepting this with grace, and even gratitude. Celibacy, with its various meanings, has always been an honourable choice for Christians. In the past, for women particularly, it offered a way in to the life of the mind and to the possibility of exercising some degree of authority in a world over-dominated by men. There have always been dedicated, creative women who have realised that they have a better chance of developing the image in a collegial relationship with men than in a married relationship, which might have denied them their personhood.

At times, and particularly in the Roman Catholic Church, celibacy has been regarded as a superior way. Many have entered religious life seeking to be more perfect than others. Celibates have advertised their way of life to the world as a special and favoured way, and have left everyone else feeling rather ordinary and spiritually inadequate. Some have entered religious life before becoming sexually aware, and have been encouraged to deny and repress any emerging sexual feelings. Today the claims of the celibate are becoming more humble, and more realistic. Celibates are sexual people, with real desires and needs. Many grow to discover that the call to complete the image of God is just as binding on them; they too are baptised into the name of the threefold God, and share the vocation to 'be fruitful and multiply'. Sex and desire will not leave us alone, whatever our choices and preferences, and honest celibates have to find ways of coming to terms with this. Desire is what provokes us to seek completion in God, and it is much more securely rooted in our nature than any *theology* of sex or desire!

For some celibates sexual desire can be projected on to God. God then becomes the object of passionate longing and the hidden life of the self with the Lord is seen as a 'mystic marriage'. The Virgin Mother of God sometimes carries imagery of completion for male celibates. The fractured image is healed by the imagery of completion which is evoked through prayer. Most celibates find, however, that though they are wholehearted in their desire to be true to God alone, they still have ordinary human needs for warmth and affection. God is not solitary, and our longing for relationship belongs to the part of us which reflects God's threefold nature.

God is God, and not a mere substitute for earthly love. But God is present in attraction and desire, in fulfilment, in brokenness and loss, and in the ache of love unfulfilled. Indeed a growing awareness of the need for closeness, for a 'significant other', may be a sign that the true fractures are coming into awareness and being mourned, and that there is a chance of healing a human hurt by human means. For some who are vowed to religious life this movement will be contained by warm friendship. Others will find that friendship opens out into sexual desire, with all the divided loyalties and complications and hard choices that follow. No human choice is easy or without temptation, and the besetting danger for celibates is emotional irresponsibility, either to those they love or to the community to which they belong. Yet the celibate way is a good way for those who can choose it freely. It functions as a sign that marriage is not compulsory. It offers a special kind of freedom from the oppressiveness that creeps into normal relationships between men and women. It reminds everyone that God is God, at the end and beginning of our deepest desires.

Homosexuality

The Church has also recognized celibacy and rejoiced in its fruits. It has not been so generous to those who are homosexual. In fact homosexuality is still widely regarded in Church circles as either a perversion, or an illness, or a kind of handicap. None of these descriptions seem to fit the experience of those who know they long for completion through an intimate relationship, but find they can only be truly intimate with one of their own sex. So there is a real problem for the Church in this area. Recent Roman Catholic teaching insists that homosexuality is an intrinsic evil; in some other Church teaching it is assumed that those who regard themselves as homosexual are simply mistaken and could be cured.

Perhaps the Church cannot celebrate these relationships, or allow them to be seen as God-given, because of its investment in marriage. Some of the fear and dread that so-called normal people feel towards homosexuals surely arises from simple envy. Homosexual love is often more intense, more fraught and more emotional in character than married love. Marriage sets people a task. It is a good task, the creation of a family, but a hard and absorbing one. Intimacy can be eroded by the practical problems of family life. Couples do not make time to talk to one another and communication becomes perfunctory. Homosexual love (especially when it comes with two incomes and no children!) can seem like a luxury. But it isn't of course. There are happy homosexuals and unhappy ones. Some rejoice in their freedom, others envy the security of marriage and its social acceptability. Many long for children. It is harder for homosexuals to be rooted in ordinariness, in the tasks of home-building and mutual responsibility, though the most successful homosexual relationships do seem to be those that involve a joint task or vision outside the emotional tie. But the Church at present seems unable to accept the possibility of a homosexual way to completion in God. It crudely assumes that homosexual love inevitably means cruel and destructive promiscuity. Sometimes it does of course, but instead of helping homosexuals to mature ways of loving the Church prefers its homosexual members to be blocked in their spiritual and emotional growth by guilt and desperation. It would rather meet the gay man weeping in the confessional after a sordid and possibly dangerous one night stand than encourage him to build a sustaining, intimate relationship. Depressed and repressed homosexuals can then be pitied and ministered unto and even admired without threatening the Church's investment in marriage.

Perhaps the Church will finally find its way towards recognizing that there are those who are simply made by God to love one of their own sex. Perhaps this leap of imagination into reality is beyond what the institutional Church can manage.

Personally I believe that both celibates and homosexuals have an essential place in God's plan. In their different ways they challenge the normative order of this world with its built-in oppressions.

Celibates do so by reminding us that God is God. I need their witness to help me acknowledge my own need for aloneness and self-possession. They speak to me of dignity in singleness and bereavement, and warn me not to sell myself short by allowing myself to be dominated or subdued by others. They are also a sign that our development as human beings is for a purpose beyond the order of this present world. Homosexuals reveal to us something about androgyny. They remind us that we are all, in some sense, male and female and our completion involves making peace between the two halves of the image when it appears to us to be fractured between its male and female aspects. It may seem strange and repellent that some seek the other half of the image in the same. But it is still the *other* that they seek unless they are purely narcissistic. They bear witness to the healing power of friendship and to the faithfulness that can bring individuals to maturity against the odds.

When we make cruel judgements against those who differ from us we do ourselves damage. For, in some sense, we need the wisdom of all three ways.

The vocation of love
Love remains the vocation of all who are baptised, and love is a sign of God to the whole community. Yet love hurts. Here it is that some of us make our most costly mistakes. Here it is often that our personal story looks most wobbly and incomplete. Here it is, also, that we come to know God not only as our Creator, but as our redeemer, our lover, the hound of heaven who will not let us go. Grace is mysteriously written even into the tragic elements of our story. Often people are compulsively attracted to those who do them emotional harm. It is as though they know the source of their own wounding, and are compelled to re-visit it in the hope of finding relief. Sometimes the desire is sound, and a small dose of emotional poison effects a dramatic cure. Wounding and healing go together. Love makes us fools before it makes us wise:

> I shall go down
> to the lovers' well

and wash this wound
that will not heal.[4]

I think of C. S. Lewis, that brilliant and abrasive apologist for
the Christian faith. From an early age Lewis cultivated the
persona that was to become a crusty academic bachelor. He
described himself, as many hurt people do, as a 'spectator' on
life rather than a player. Before his conversion to Christianity
he seems to have had a strange long term secret affair with a
widow. In late middle age he fell catastrophically in love with
an American divorcee. She was eminently unsuitable for him,
and yet they were intensely happy, until her tragic death from
cancer. That love and loss changed Lewis and in a sense he was
never the same again. His once rather glib faith darkened and
deepened as he lost many of his certainties: 'In the only life we
know God hurts us beyond our worst fears and beyond all we
can imagine.'[5] Lewis's image of himself as self-sufficient was
cracked for ever. And yet he sees the hand of God in the
process even when God seems to be working for his hurt: 'O
God, O God why did you take such trouble to force this
creature out of its shell if it is now doomed to crawl back – to
be sucked back – into it?'[6]

Lewis was broken, but he was not sucked back into his well-
defended shell. In his last years he seems to have been known
as a kinder, more patient human being. When he was frail
with various disabilities he wrote to an American correspon-
dent who was fraught with illness and fear: 'The best way to
cope with mental debility and total inertia is to submit to it
entirely. Don't *try* to concentrate. Pretend you are a dormouse
or even a turnip'.[7] And so on, with gentle wit and sympathy.
A few months later he died.

The cost of love

Grief is the cost of love, over and over again. If we are capable
of love we may have to die many times and know the

[4] Geoffrey Hill, 'The Pentecost Castle', from *Tenebrae*, André Deutsch, 1978.
[5] C. S. Lewis, *A Grief Observed*, Faber, 1961, p. 24.
[6] ibid. p. 18.
[7] *Letters to an American Lady*, Hodder and Stoughton, 1969, p. 116.

crucifixion of desire and its rebirth. As tradition reminds us, the cross is the one thing of which we can be sure in this life, 'our one reliance'.[8] Human passion and divine desire meet and mingle here. From the Saviour's side come water and blood. Our all too human grief and failure are contained within the divine heartbreak. It is for that purpose that the child of God is sent from the home of the Trinity; Abraham's table is already an altar, and the chalice rests on it, offered outwards. We are witnesses and imitators of the love of God whenever we endure human heartbreak. St John of the Cross reminds us that 'we must not be without our cross, even as our beloved had his cross until he died the death of love'.[9]

Marriage, celibacy and priesthood are all traditional ways of life that involve a kind of martyrdom. So are the compromises and the fractured choices in which many of us live today. All, in different ways, break us and heal us at the same time. Through death we come to life, like the Christian martyrs who have hoped in resurrection. Martyrdom is a dangerous and unpopular word. It reminds us that there is a Christian pathology, and it is sadistic and masochistic. Those who invest in martyrdom, the perfectionists and narcissists and workaholics already 'have their reward', like the Pharisees.

But there is another kind of martyrdom which, though it is inevitable, is not chosen. It is the suffering that accompanies any form of real love, the desolation that travels with desire. For to want is to want from my wounded centre, from where I am not free, but in need.

Some Christian traditions have separated *agape* (selfless love) from *eros* (desire), and have encouraged believers to make war on desire. But this only worsens the fracture of the image, causing us to identify with an ideal self who is not us and cannot be intimate with others or with God.

Agape and *eros* need each other. And to love I must have access to both, and let both inform each other. This is where it hurts. Desire cannot always be fulfilled. Selfless love cannot always reach across the gap which separates lover from beloved. If I love I must respect the mystery of the beloved. A

---

[8] 'O cross our one reliance, hail', from the hymn of Venantius Fortunatus, *Vexilla Regis Prodeunt.*
[9] *Letter 9.*

person who is loved has the right to withdraw and refuse, to wait, to suffer, to seek, and, sometimes, to hate.

How can I know you if you are not yourself with me? How can you know me if I don't show you who I am? The fire of God tests me to be true in my desiring, and to be faithful to what desires me. Love learns to make love at the table of the Trinity where the three beings are both separate in form and free to greet one another.

The martyrdom of love is the furnace of fire in which God tests us. God does not test us to find out if we are true, but to help us to self-knowledge and humility. When our deepest desires are kindled we are very vulnerable. Our true selves and our inherited and personal sin reveal themselves as intertwined, death and life contending together.

Sickness and sexuality

That is why there are elements of sickness in all marriages, and in all homosexual relationships, and in all the adjustments of celibacy. We can see the sicknesses in the paths we have not chosen, but not in our own. It is much easier for the married to see sexual sickness, say, in hair shirts and spiked bracelets taken on to mortify than in the casual cruelty of word and deed that might exist in an otherwise satisfactory relationship. The hierarchy of a celibate church can see sickness in the homosexual state, but not in the casual inhumanity with which it presumes to dictate the sex lives of millions of married couples. Homosexuals are often bitter against the Church, but are far less incisive in their criticisms of harmful or promiscuous practices within the gay community.

Our anxiety about sex forces itself outwards and projects its own guilt and shame on to others. Part of the Christian task is to interpret this anxiety. I find myself having to own my own ambivalence about intimacy. I desire and fear that closeness to another human being in which I know and am known. And the desire and fear come from the threefold God who has made me to share in his image.

Knowing Jesus

At the heart of Christian faith is an invitation to be close to Jesus Christ, to know him and be known by him. It is on the night of his betrayal, according to tradition, that he offers himself to us in the most intimate words and gestures. Our eucharistic rituals express, and mercifully mask, the beauty and terror of what God offers us in Jesus. He comes to us in the memory of the flesh, in the body and the blood, offering his true substance without reserve. There are profound sexual overtones in this. To receive and share in the body and blood of Jesus is to be implicated in the passion of our God, in the joyful suffering and desire of the Trinity. We live and die at the point of breaking, of fracture. Here it is that we are delivered up, with Jesus, and pass over into the hands of the Father.

We have no control over the outcome of this surrender. The vows of a lifetime, the promises of lovers, can be broken, but they cannot be unsaid. They can change their meaning, but they cannot be unsaid. Jesus had no control over the outcome of his dying. He died in utter loss. But in spite of and because of that he is raised by the Father.

In the same way to bear the true cross which is revealed to us through our wounded sexuality is to become open to the possibility of resurrection. This is the Christian way, as the creeds assure us. From the point of acceptance I can 'look to' (not having reached) 'the resurrection of the dead and the life of the world to come'.

Summary

On the sixth day God creates men and women in his image and after his likeness. We are commissioned to populate and manage the earth. I argue that the image of God is not in the mind alone, but also in our sexuality. The task that God gives us can only be fulfilled by men and women working together.

But deeper things are going on. Here, the Bible struggles with its language, and in its struggle later writers found a mirror of the doctrine of the Trinity. We mirror God in so far as we are not self-sufficient and isolated, but needing and giving and in relationship. Two meditations follow, based on two pictures; Rublev's icon of the Trinity, and Picasso's 'The Tragedy'.

These suggest two rather different models of the image of God, one which suggests its integrity, the other which describes its fragmentation.

The challenge to our prayers is that Jesus invites us to wholeness. The classic way is through marriage, which we reflect on. Another honoured way is through celibacy. We look at some of the advantages and dangers of that route. A third way, I suggest, is homosexuality, but this is so unacceptable to the Church that it is a particularly hard way to follow at present. I still believe however, that it is possible. Also that the three ways need to enrich each other. Love is the goal and the road. We look at the cost of love in grief, and the knowledge of sickness which must be part of coming to sexual and spiritual integrity. We also consider what it means to accept the invitation to 'know Jesus', given that we are bodily, and sexual, creatures.

Suggestions for prayer

1 Look at the descriptions of Rublev's 'The Trinity' and Picasso's 'The Tragedy' (pp. 92–4). Which moves you more? Make your reaction the subject of a conversation with God.

2 Spend some time thinking about your parents. How did they help or hinder the way the image of God is forming in you? Pray for the healing of the parts of yourself that you feel or think are damaged in some way. You might use this verse of a hymn to the Holy Spirit as a prayer:

> What is soiled, make thou pure,
> What is wounded, work its cure;
> What is parched, fructify;
> What is rigid, gently bend;
> What is frozen, warmly tend;
> Straighten what goes erringly.[10]

[10]

Veni Sancte Spiritus, tr. J. M. Neale (English Hymnal), usually attributed to Stephen Langton, the thirteenth-century Archbishop of Canterbury.

3 Work out how you would pray for someone whose sexual desire orientation is different from your own. Then do it!

4 Try to remember your first awareness of your own gender, as a boy or a girl. Draw or write down who was around at the time. Where was God for you that day? Invite God into the picture as you see him now. What does he say to you now you have grown up to be a mature man or woman?

5 Pray for the well-being of the person closest to you, the most significant other person in your life. It doesn't, of course, have to be a person with whom you have a sexual relationship, though it may well be. Thank God for what that relationship means to you. If there is no one 'significant other' in your life ask the Lord to show you how he is making the image of God come to maturity within you.

6 Read 1 Samuel 18:1–5, which describes the relationship between David and Jonathan. Remember an occasion in your life when you have been moved by the loyalty of a friend. How has God shown loyalty to you?

7 Look again at the pictures on pp. xi and xii. Which picture comes closest to expressing how you feel about yourself and your relationships with others and with God? Pray with your own answer, asking God to reveal himself to you as the God of joy, suffering and healing.

Day Seven

The Sleeping Lord[1]

Thus the heavens and the earth were finished, and all their multitude. And on the seventh day God finished the work that he had done, and he rested on the seventh day from all the work that he had done. So God blessed the seventh day and hallowed it, because on it God rested from all the work that he had done in creation. (Gen. 2:1–3)

On the seventh day God finished his work and rested.

God's rest

The authors of the creation account complete their narrative with a divine pause. God stops. Until this point we have been dazzled by descriptions of the holy art of cosmic engineering. Now the engineer, as it were, steps back and takes a snooze. What is going on?

For six days we have witnessed the power, energy and magic of God. We see the works of the Lord in our living planet and the night sky. We *are* the works of the Lord. We see patience, experiment, calculation. We see change. We see shape, space, form and time. Nothingness is ruptured to allow the possibility of consciousness. The deep is torn to allow for safe space. Here, God tosses in the chance of life. Here, God honours time and its wounds. Now God plays with the wild creatures. Now God invents tame and domestic and intelligent ones. There is structure, form, discipline and the ordering and

---

[1] This chapter heading is stolen from the title of a poem by David Jones which is set in the Celtic world in Roman times. See *The Sleeping Lord*, Faber and Faber, 1974.

110

re-ordering of simple and beautiful forms. All this is the work of God's ingenious and inventive word. It is made up like a poem or song out of God's head, improvising on what is already there.

Sometimes the work of creation is presented as though it were a huge and complicated scenic construction which culminates in the dramatic entrance of man as principal actor. But that is to ignore the interconnectedness of all the different parts, and the involvement of God with the non-human creation. The culmination of God's work is not on the sixth day, but on the seventh. The seventh day is the clue to the divine work because it is the day of meanings. God looks at the astonishing universe and calls the seventh day blessed. I find this rather refreshing. It suggests that God is capable of relaxation as well as work, and is not so anxious about the universe that he needs to be doing things to it all the time. In contrast, the rather relentless God of our well-trained Christian imagination *never* stops:

> Unresting, unhasting and silent as light
> nor wanting, nor wasting, thou rulest in might.

This God is a workaholic who is ceaselessly pouring more and more of himself, his will, his purpose, into his creation. He is endlessly unsatisfied. The God of Genesis on the other hand stands back from what has been made and takes a break. God rests. God enjoys. And God makes it a rule of the busy universe that rest and passivity should be built in as the most essential part of the timetable. The seventh day is sacred time, playtime and the heart of time. It is the key to time because it is about completion. Work, then, for God, is not an end in itself.

Blessed idleness

I think it is important to remember this because we are all, to some extent, scarred by the consequences of a ruthless work ethic, as a result of which we have forgotten what work is for. Work is not for more work. It is for blessing. The idea that work is blessed *in itself* is a heresy to which Christians are peculiarly attached. How many endlessly shining stoves and floors, how many neurotically clean carpets, how many never-to-be-wound-up committees are the consequences of Christian perfectionism, which would always rather find something that needs doing than face the question why. Of course work is necessary. It is part of our task to manage the planet. Of course it is absorbing. But without proper rest we are cut off from ourselves. We become slaves of, and addicts to, our own powers. Rest gives meaning to work, just as work makes rest necessary.

So God does not bless the first six days. He is too busy. He blesses some of the creatures that he produces. But the work itself is not blessed, it is said and done. The blessing is in the completion, in the finished work, in the sacred time at the end. So the famous catch-phrase of monastic life, *laborare est orare*, 'work is prayer', needs looking at critically. The point of work is completion, and it might be more accurate to add, 'but rest is blessed'!

The Sabbath

This is recognised much more fully among Jews than it is among Christians. The Jewish work ethic is as demanding and rigorous as any. Yet the claims of the Sabbath are absolute over the religious Jew. Work is part of the human task before God but it is the Sabbath which is blessed. The Sabbath is a complete break, a space for worship, for eating and drinking and play. Above all, the Sabbath celebrates the life of the home and the relationships within the family.

It worries me that Christians are encouraged to wear themselves out for God, to live at the point of exhaustion, as if it were a virtuous thing to do. Committed Christians are often expected to show their commitment by spending their free time in Church activities. Weekends become as pressing as weekdays. Time and talents are all treated as commodities, to be used in God's great goodness-producing factory. Total commitment to God is interpreted as endless doing, for sacred-sounding ends such as 'The Church' or 'The Kingdom'. Lives are stretched and strained, and sometimes even sacrificed, for religious ideals. When it is assumed that such sacrifices are an appropriate response to God, the whole idea of real leisure and enjoyment induces guilt.

People exhaust themselves in order to feel that they genuinely deserve a holiday and that their need for time off is legitimate. Holidays and time off are not seen as holydays, carnivals, but as necessary space in which to recharge our batteries for the *real* task of our lives, which is to be socially and spiritually productive. So deeply have we all been influenced by this sort of thinking that many of us feel guilty about taking time off and, when we do, become quite anxious and depressed. The lifting of tasks leaves us internally empty and desolate, and we find we are unable to enjoy free time as a normal part of life. Yet by making the seventh day holy God seems to be saying something about the need for genuine balance in our lives. We need to be able to move freely and thankfully between work and rest, activity and passivity. This faces all of us with different problems and possibilities, which need to be part of our praying. How do we get the balance right?

A rhythm of work and rest

An evening hymn by an Anglican contemplative suggests the essential spiritual value of rest. It is not just recovery time, it is a place where God's glory is revealed

> We praise you Father for your gift
> of dusk and nightfall over earth
> foreshadowing the mystery
> of death that leads to endless day.
>
> Within your hands we rest secure
> in quiet sleep our strength renew
> yet give your people hearts that wake
> in love to you, unsleeping Lord.
>
> Your glory may we ever seek
> in rest as in activity
> until its fullness is revealed
> O source of life, O Trinity.[2]

---

[2] Hymn sung at Compline by the Benedictine nuns of St Mary's Abbey, West Malling.

It is good to notice here that night is seen as a gift, which foreshadows death as a positive promise. Sleep renews strength, but it is also a place for going down into the glory of God. When we sleep we are very vulnerable. God, the unsleeping Lord, watches us with love, knowing us differently from our daytime selves. The life of the Trinity is a rhythmic life of work and rest, doing and being, a life of creativity and passivity. So the art for us is to learn about these things from God.

Time boundaries and working roles

The institution of the Sabbath suggests a clear boundary between work and rest. It suggests that it is part of God's grace to make this distinction for us. In practice, the boundaries between the two often need some formalising and protecting. This is more complicated for Christians than it is for Jews. We are not committed to keeping the Jewish Sabbath. Sunday, the day of resurrection is *not* the Sabbath, it is the first day of God's working week! Yet the Sabbath principle remains. It is, as Jesus said, 'made for humankind' (Mark 2:27), and without it we become less than human. God has made us to need both work and rest, and the boundaries between them.

We can get some grasp on what this means by thinking about what the boundaries keep apart. The world of work is usually a public world, a world of engagement, activity, productivity and decision. The world of rest is more likely to be a private world, intimate or alone, or peopled with chosen companions.

In the public world we are required to fulfil roles. In the private world we are more likely to relax a little and be more unreservedly ourselves. The roles we play in the public world are not false. If they are we will find ourselves living under intolerable strain. Our roles are not false, but neither are they the whole of us. If we are in balance the roles we play are appropriate and necessary, but they leave part of us behind.

The second account of creation, which follows in the rest of Genesis 2, describes how God protects his human creatures as they are driven from the garden of Eden on their long journey through this world.

Adam and Eve are sent out into a world in which they are

going to have to work. But God mercifully clothes them in animal skins that will keep them warm and safe in the wild. I think this means that the world of tasks and work requires the protection of the roles that God gives us. Instead of animal skins, God, as it were, sews cassocks and dog collars for the clergy, uniforms for policemen, nurses and pilots and overalls for sculptors, car mechanics and plumbers. We are not to work all the time from our place of vulnerability. God gives us, in our tasks, the forms of protection that we need against chaos. And this includes not only uniforms, but forms of behaviour. When I worked as a television producer I took on some of the formal defences and boundaries that I gradually learnt went with the job. I discovered about the joys and sorrows of working in teams. I paid attention to the hierarchies of power. I tried, not always successfully, to be diplomatic, which meant that I sometimes bit my tongue, and did not always tell the whole of the truth to everybody. I consulted others when I thought it necessary, and tried to keep my own counsel when that seemed more important. Appropriate, learned behaviours helped me to acquire both the freedom and the authority I needed to get programmes on to the television screen. Many of these skills have transferred well to working in the Church. But there have been new things to learn. Wearing clerical dress for the first time was a bit of a shock. People look at you with expectations. Gushing smiles, nervousness, hostility, or just a kind of complicit recognition. The uniform evokes expectations, and many clergy try to live up to them. In jobs that are only partly congenial it is relatively easy to keep the balance between work and rest. The working role is taken off at the end of the working day, and the recreation of home, television, the pub or whatever, fills out the rest of the person.

It is much harder when our deep motivations are involved with our work, especially when we are not aware of them. Some of us are driven by a need for power and visibility in the world. When we are not working we feel powerless and invisible. Others need to be needed, and find it embarrassing and exposing to have to switch off from others to consider their own real needs. Others find the fear of not having enough money forces them to work harder than they should or, sometimes, than they need to. Some are dependent on the *image* that their role carries to themselves and to society, and feel lost and diminished without it. And then there are those who live alone, or are unhappily married, who get most of their contacts and friendship from work. Free time, for them, is often a desert of loneliness.

This is why unemployment is a spiritual problem as well as an economic one. Long term unemployment makes people feel cut off from their God-given task, and the proper protection that goes with it. The sense of powerlessness and lack of energy and purpose can be devastating. 'Resting' is necessary, but we all know what the actor means when he says it is what he is doing. Eternal rest is not for now, though if we are very depressed it may seem a pleasing prospect.

When protection goes too far

So for all these reasons it is sometimes hard to remember that we are more than our working roles. The knowledge of the intimacy and pain that accompany times of rest may even cause us to shudder. We want our defences against the garden of bliss, the seductions of the snake and the hope of heaven.

Professional roles are the best protections because they are subtle and all-pervasive. The behaviour and attitudes which go with church jobs are hugely successful defences against pain or intimacy. They encourage clergy and ministers to live at second hand, secretly feeding off the hurts of others, while feeling virtuous in their detachment. I am always rather cheered when a professional carer admits to feeling bored, fed up, amused, frightened or infatuated by one of his or her clients! At least it means there might be a person underneath the mask, who is having interesting and subversive desires and thoughts. For there is a terrible price to pay for identifying ourselves too seriously with our roles. *From* our armour we may operate successfully in a hostile and dangerous world, but we can know nothing *inside* the armour except our own fragility and emptiness. No one can come near us, and we cannot come near anyone else.

To identify wholly with our roles is to lose our inner selves. To do so when God is calling us to rest and intimacy is to betray a deep lack of trust in God, and a lack of insight that God is a God of joy. We are anxious about ourselves and our place in the universe, and so we make God in our image as an anxious God, a busybody God, who spies on us to see if we are using our time and talents efficiently, and clobbers us with illness or disaster if we don't come up to scratch.

Working without defences

One thing which might help us is to learn from those whose roles in the world require a certain tough vulnerability, a laying down of defences. When I worked for the BBC I made a film[3] about a hospice. I met doctors and nurses who have developed the medical skills to help with the discomfort and disability that usually go with much advanced cancer. I also met patients suffering from cancer and other diseases and their families. I quickly learned that in the last stages of the disease sheer professionalism is not enough. What patients need is human warmth and honesty. Sheila Cassidy, who was at that time the Director of St Luke's Hospice in Plymouth, spoke in the film of what her role was when there was nothing more that could be done. Then the only task left is to be a companion to the dying person. Being alongside them, with empty hands, with nothing to give except for one's presence. As I began to prepare for pastoral ministry I realized that there were occasions when I needed to be able to learn to be alongside people without being able to do anything that would make them better or happier. There are times when *presence* is all you have to offer. This can make you feel shy and awkward and vulnerable, because we all like to feel that we can *do* something in the presence of suffering. But sometimes there is nothing to be done except to 'hang on in there'.

A similar undefendedness is also an inevitable part of good mothering, of art, and of contemplative prayer. All these human commitments involve real work and tasks. But they also involve an essential passivity at the heart of doing which is partly quietness, partly playfulness, partly vigilance, and partly just being *with*. It may be being with a person, an idea, oneself or God. People who act from passivity in this way take the Sabbath of God into the working world as a witness and sign that God is God. A neurotic and anxious world will undervalue them and not see what they are doing or why. Full-time

[3] *The Loneliest Journey*, an Everyman film for BBC TV.

mothers, artists and contemplatives do not appear to contribute much to the economy of free enterprise capitalism. But
they are contributing to the total human economy of work
and rest. They are also witnessing to the joy of God as much as
a saint or a bird or an acrobat. Not that they are special. They
too need time off. Time doing something different. If they
don't get it they will 'burn out'. What they need to do that is
different may be quite active, intellectually stimulating or
repetitive, or it may involve them in playing a deliberate role
which puts back some of the protection that has been worn
away in being *with*. Contemplative nuns wear the most formal
habits, and perhaps they need to! For it is emotionally draining
and exposing to work from a place of attentiveness. No one
should do it always or for ever. Mothers who return to work
after years of bringing up children often find it gives them a
tremendous boost in self-confidence to rediscover that they
can take on a working role.

A God of work and rest

God desires to know us in our true strengths and in our
weakness. God works, and then rests. This is theologically and
spiritually important. A God who is only at rest is a detached
God who rejects the creativity of work. We can only know
such a God by silence and dying. A God who can *only* work is
a slave-driver, an insecure God whose demands on us are
endless. Going on from this we can see that God comes to us,
as so often, under two kinds. God comes to us in our strength.
God protects and confirms us, giving us tasks and roles. But
God also seeks to know us in our vulnerability. The Lord
desires to know us unmasked, in the place where we hurt and
need.

   God gets to know us by passivity as well as activity. God
stands back, and, by resting, allows us to become artists and
shapers and managers of this world. God lets us take risks,
suffering our incompetencies and mistakes. For passivity leaves
God open and vulnerable. God does not guard himself against
his universe with legions of angels. God leaves room, by
resting, to be acted on by the creation. God wants and wills to
be on the receiving end of creation. Like any lover he longs
to be desired as well as to desire. So God rests, trusting himself

to all the wild and dangerous and beautiful and disappointing possibilities that he has created.

God's desire to be human

God wants to know what it is to be human. That means knowing what it is like to be sad and lonely and tired and unconfident, as well as what it is like to be strong. God wants to renew our faith in ourselves. This is why our tradition tells us that Christ, the Word and true image of the Father, is born among the beasts and raised from among the dead. God rests in the world of our making, just as we rest in the world of divine activity. In Jesus Christ God rests in the same kind of poverty as all human beings pass through; the poverty of birth, of infancy, of dependency. We can hold him, touch him, cuddle him, and not be afraid. He is the child of our desire, the one who draws out our love. But the baby in the manger grows up, and then we know him in his strength. The child of Mary grows to be the gifted young man, the teacher, the healer, the prophet of Israel. He is the active, creative Word of God made flesh. Then *we* are on the receiving end, we are exposed and unmasked and find ourselves trying to listen, trying to understand, trying to learn to acknowledge the truth of our sin and God's love for us, trying to learn what it means to love and forgive one another, to suffer and be with. But the young man makes enemies. And then we know him in the poverty of his failure. We know him in helplessness that we cannot help. We know him in rejection, and we are part of what rejects him. We hold him to persuade him, to restrain him. We kiss him to betray him. We judge him and kill him. He is passive to our violence. He dies on the cross and rests in the grave on the dark Sabbath of Easter Eve.

What I think is happening in the Christian story is that God is offering me the companionship of his human experience, and lets me share, though dimly and inadequately, in the divine wisdom. God comes to make his home with me and calls me to make my home with him. There is rest and work, activity and passivity, desiring and being desired, on both sides.

At home with God

On a visit to Bethlehem in 1983 I bought a set of carved wooden nativity figures from an olive wood factory. There are two sheep, two oxen, one shepherd, three wise men, Joseph, Mary, the crib and the infant Jesus. There was nothing special about them. They were like thousands and thousands of similar sets made and sold each year.

I have always liked to have them around me, not only at Christmas, but all year round. These little pieces of carved wood represent to me God's 'house of bread' – for which the Hebrew name is Bethlehem. They remind me of the poverty of God and of God's endless gift of himself to me. They remind me also that Christ lives in the poor members of my inner household, and that I can only find him if I seek him in my poverty, with my defences down. I lost a sheep once, down the back of a bookcase. The one remaining sheep looked odd and out of balance. I grieved for the lost sheep and rejoiced when I found it. It was as though I had lost and found part of myself. At Christmas I often put a candle with the wooden Bethlehem, and it becomes a visual focal point. Looking at the figures I realise that I am looking with my inner eye towards a God who rests and plays, a God who wills to be known as a child-God, a God who delights.

Bethlehem – house of bread

Our child God is born in Bethlehem. But Bethlehem is not fairyland. It is not where the rainbow ends or the home of the Wizard of Oz. Bethlehem is a real place with a present and a past. When I used to go there frequently to make television programmes it was a place of tinsel and cameras, dusty candles and machine-guns. The electric bulbs that formed a garland round the cross at the Church of the Nativity came on at dusk but only half of them worked. In the shrine that commemorates the Nativity, the official birthplace of Jesus, the votive lamps were meticulously divided between the Armenians, the Greeks and the Catholics. Protocol was all. Woe betide the film producer who tried to smuggle a camera in without letters of permission from the Armenian Patriarch, the Greek Patriarch and the Roman Catholic Franciscan Provincial! All must agree, and agree that the others have agreed, and agree to appear or not appear together. The perils of ecclesiastical one-upmanship had to be prevented by eternal vigilance. Tourists and pilgrims crowded around in stripy shirts and sunhats, squinting through the dark, adjusting their Nikons, saying the rosary, yawning and fidgeting, praying. And muddled up with the squalor and piety and strife there is the divine mystery which howls in the night with a voice of hunger, needing human love.

In recent years Bethlehem has become a place of desolation, conflict and danger. Christians have departed in droves and tourists and pilgrims are often too scared to go, or are put off by the endless security checks. The Church of the Nativity was besieged for weeks in the Palestinian *intifada* when gunmen took refuge within it. Its ancient walls were damaged by gunfire. Yet it remains a holy place, a symbol as well as a location. Monks and nuns and scholars have prayed here and studied here. In the fourth century of the Christian era the terrible St Jerome lived here, the brilliant Bible scholar and arch-misogynist. If he can become a saint, anyone can, for he was a caustic and irritable character with few natural advantages apart from his tenacious intelligence. On the seventh day God rested. The world is not changed. Our world has terrors as the ancient world did. Our world has its share of human and natural violence: suicide bombers, catastrophic floods and earthquakes, the nuclear threat, endless hunger, horrific cancers and AIDS. Yet God wills to be on the receiving end of this world, and he trusts himself to it, in the sleeping child of Bethlehem. That is why we come, again and again, to the manger of Jesus, whether in Bethlehem or in the heart. All are welcome here. The beasts and the shepherd, the sheep and the wise men, Joseph and Mary. All creation worships here as the Lord sleeps and cries in helplessness. Here at Bethlehem, in this seedy little town, the whole human story is manifest in miniature. This is what the early fathers meant when they spoke of the recapitulation of creation. The eternal Word of God, through whom the heavens were made, is born in time. He is 'knitted' as the carol[4] says 'to man's nature'.

---

[4] 'Thus was I knit to man's nature/to call my true love to the dance', 'My Dancing Day', traditional carol. See *The Oxford Book of Carols*, OUP, 1975, no. 71.

And this, as the medieval scholars knew, as the fathers and mothers of the early Church knew, is how he saves us. St Bernard of Clairvaux was a formidable scholar and reformer. He revived and restored the ascetic Cistercian Order, he wrote stern letters to popes, he got involved in all the political and ecclesiastical squabbles of his time. Yet he knew that an ability to rest and be still lies at the heart of both the human and the divine endeavour. God's love is shown in the child, the little one, who cannot harm us but needs us: 'His infant state demonstrates how easy it is to please him. Everyone knows how easily a child forgives'.[5]

Commenting on that passage the nineteenth-century theologian Gioacchino Ventura says:

> We are poor, we have little or nothing to give. Yet, if only we want to – we can become worthy to be reconciled to God through this Child ... Not that this reconciliation can ever happen without repentance, but our mere repentance would be a very tiny thing to merit divine pardon ... We must, accordingly, take from him to supply for our indigence: we shall take his little body in our hands as though it were our own. Since he is born of our stock, it is our very own as it is written: 'A child is born to us and a son is given to us' (Isa. 9:6).[6]

To 'take this little body into our hands' is to link Christmas with the Eucharist. It is to come empty handed to the table of the Trinity, where bread is offered and shared. This is where we find him, and always will. In the house of bread, under the night stars, among the beasts.

Summary
In this last chapter I have been looking at the seventh day, on which God rested. The implications of this is that there is a rhythm of work and rest within God's life. God has made the rest time quite fundamental to our well-being by blessing the

[5] St Bernard, 1, *On the Epiphany*.
[6] From Gioacchino Ventura, 'Le Bellezze della Fede', tr. Sr. Mary Ursula Blake, SHCJ, Source, no. 3, Summer 1972.

seventh day. We must take this seriously by finding the right balance between work and rest in our own lives. To do this we need to think about the roles that accompany work, and how they protect us in certain ways. We can learn from those who, in some sense, work from a place of passivity.

God's rest has further significance for us. It shows his willingness to be at the receiving end of our activity, and to know us from the inside, in our weakness as well as our strength. The rest of the chapter is a meditation on the incarnation and on the meaning of Bethlehem as the place where God rests in our midst, showing his need for us, and acceptance of us.

Suggestions for prayer

1 'I lie down and sleep; I wake again, for the Lord sustains me' (Ps. 3:5). How does the Lord sustain you in your sleep? Imagine yourself at the age of six, tired and fast asleep in bed. Where is God? Make your answer the subject of a conversation with God.

2 Read the story of Jesus asleep in the storm, in Mark 6:45–51. Stay with the story in quiet attentiveness and notice what it suggests to you about the storms and calms in your own life.

3 Make a list of five positive things about your working role. Ask God how he meets you in your working world, what he expects of you, and what he has given you to enable you to fulfil your tasks for him.

4 Make a list of five activities, pleasures, places or ways of being which relax and refresh you. Ask God how he shares them with you. When did you last really enjoy yourself? Make your answer the subject of a conversation with God.

5 'Those who wait for the Lord shall renew their strength' (Isa. 40:31). Wait for the Lord, by being quiet and attentive for ten or twenty minutes, repeating the words of this text to yourself.

6 Do some physical activity (swimming, jogging, walking) which relaxes and refreshes you. Pray as you do so using a favourite phrase from the Bible or the line of a hymn.

7 In your imagination go to the stable of Bethlehem, and join

Mary, Joseph, the sheep, the shepherds, the oxen, and the wise men. Have you brought anything with you? What is it? What do you hope to find? If it seems appropriate, choose the verse of a Christmas hymn or a carol and say it as a prayer.

Epilogue

So where have we travelled in these days of praying with Genesis? At the end of this book it would be good if we could add our own commentary to the Genesis text, a commentary which would tell of our own life story and what we have discovered of the work of God in creating us. The end of the Bible gives us a picture of heaven, and promises us that if we are faithful our names will be written in the book of life, never to be forgotten by God (Rev. 20:12–15). The end of our days is not destruction, not oblivion, but completion in God.

As I work through this scripture for the last time in this book I am conscious of a need for a role model, for someone who will show me more about the pattern of creation and enable me to assimilate more of what God is showing me. The tradition provides me with such a model in the person of Mary, the mother of Jesus. The Council of Ephesus in AD 431 declared her true title to be '*theotokos*', mother of God, and so she is known in prayer and devotion. Mary does stand, in some sense, on the threshold of humanity and divinity. That is why it is appropriate to greet Mary as sister, mother and friend – and to ask for her prayers. I believe that we need Mary and that our faith is distorted without her. Only from her can I learn to bear Christ into the world, and so fulfil what God is making of me. Only through her can I give the word of God shape and form, flesh and spirit within the limitations of my own being. She is how I know God dwells with us and strives for our peace.

So we end with a summary of the seven days, in the light of what we know of the whole purpose of God, which is to know us and be known by us in a relationship of love and freedom. This may help us to see the separations and links which God is forming in our lives at the moment.

125

Day One

The first day of creation is the day of permissions. God gives the universe permission to be, to evolve itself into consciousness and communication. He makes room for what is other than himself. In the Christmas story this first day is recalled by the annunciation (Luke 1:26–38). God's angel comes to Mary bearing the divine Word. Just as the watery nothingness was stirred by the brooding Spirit of God, so Mary is 'troubled' by the angel's arrival. The waste and void were vast, unconscious, dark and simple. Mary is unknowing of what God will make of her, innocent of what will be brought to birth in her. But God does not command Mary as he commanded the light to spring from nothing. God will always work in companionship with human beings now that the universe has brought them into existence. So God greets Mary in his angel. God prophesies what will happen to her and through her. God comforts and reassures her. Like the three angels who visit Abraham, Mary's angel is friendly. Though Luke's narrative gives us only one angel it is an angel with Trinitarian style.

God began creating with the words, 'Let there be light', which put into motion the whole stream of life and consciousness in which human beings find themselves. Mary is able to recognise God's angel because she is aware of herself as God's creature. When she is named, she answers. She knows who she is, even though she is unaware of who she will become. Mary answers in words that echo God's, 'Let it be to me according to your word.' In these words, so like God's, she gives God permission to be human. In these words she becomes for us the one who is full of grace, who overflows with divine wisdom.

The beginning of our praying is hearing God's first word, allowing us to be. Then, as we grow into ourselves, we will begin to hear God naming us, not only for our own sake but for his. This is when we are troubled because we do not know what will be asked of us, or what God will bring to birth through us. This is when God greets us and comforts us, and prophesies to us what we cannot know or understand. Like Abraham's wife Sarah, we may laugh at God's audacity. Like Mary, we may consent. Either way the living God comes as our companion and our friend to share our living and dying and to ask us to share the divine life.

Day Two

On the second day of creation God creates a great space. Aeons have passed, about which we know nothing from the text of scripture. The history of the universe is not in the book of Genesis but in the cosmic dust and the spaces which surround and interpenetrate our solar system. Yet in time, and perhaps along with many other planets and living worlds, God creates this safe space in which the heaven and earth of our planet are formed. This pattern continues in the making of each one of us. We are brought to birth from the safe space of the womb. We are nurtured in the space that our parents create for us, until we are ready to stand our ground on our own feet.

Mary stands her ground before God's angel. She does not run away. She does not hide. By her consent to God Mary becomes the nurturing space in which the living God comes to birth in time: 'For in this rose contained was heaven and earth in little space.'[1]

So in our praying we need to receive from God the knowledge of our own space. We need to know our form and boundaries, to stand up to God as the selves we are, in our weakness and in our strength. Then, in exchange, when we are ready to receive him, God will ask us for permission to come and share our space with us. God will not bully or frighten, although it is not outside his range to batter the strong or to seduce the passionate.

Day Three

On the third day God creates life. This is the most risky throw of God's dice. Much could go wrong, and perhaps has in other parts of the universe, in other universes. God makes the planet green, and now there is greed, envy, competition. These are not named yet, because there is no one to name them, but the possibilities are there in the abundant and ruthless multiplications and megadeaths which begin to erupt over the earth's surface.

Mary does not refuse God. Self-possessed though she is, she is not closed to what is new and outside her experience. She

---

[1] From the carol 'There is no rose'. Medieval carol text used by Benjamin Britten in *A Ceremony of Carols*.

could have killed the angel by the power of depressive scepticism, and I'm sure it wouldn't have been the first time that
that has happened. But Mary is Jewish and she has been formed
by the Jewish scriptures. She knows that God is alive and
creative and is not bound by necessity outside his own free
will. She enters God's will by allowing herself to be filled with
the Holy Spirit. She becomes the bearer of God's life, God's
breath, God's fire. So she conceives the Word of God in her
mind and heart and womb. She makes possible the divine life
among us, the life that multiplies in blessing as it passes
through our hands.

In the same way prayer requires us to be open to the life that
God has given us. Life comes in a package to be unwrapped.
And it comes with death built in. It is green with abundance
and jealousy. It is a dangerous gift, but to refuse it is to wither
and die before we have lived. As we discover how to accept
our own life from God's hand so we come to be aware that
new possibilities are being seeded in us. These arise when we
allow ourselves to change and suffer, from our little dyings
which are rehearsals for death.

Day Four

On the fourth day God creates the stars, the signs of time.
They are far more ancient than we can imagine, yet for us they
are markers of human times that we need to remember, days
and years of significance.

Jesus is born in real human time, as St Luke reminds us,
'while Quirinius was governor of Syria' (Luke 2:2). God gives
us the freedom of living in real time. The events of our lives
really happen. We can affect the course of this world and we
are affected by what happens around us. Through Mary, the
star of Jesus rises over the human world. The infant Jesus is
linked to the royal house of David. He is the desire of nations,
and therefore the judge of kings and governments and the
refuge of all who have been exiled or injured in war or
conflict. It is to him that the wise of this world come guided
by a new star. In the nativity story they are represented by the
three wise men, who are also seen as kings.[2]

[2] See Psalm 72:10,15.

So in our praying the challenge to us is to acknowledge that we have power to act on the world, to make meanings in our lives, to encounter the living God in the events and accidents of our existence. Time gives us access to truth and healing, 'time for amendment of life', as the Shorter Prayer Book used to put it, and the chance to forgive. In this process the wise men remind us that we need every ounce of our intelligence, skill and imaginative power to weave our experience into communicable meanings. At the same time the figure of Mary stands beside us as our companion and prophet of God's infinite and motherly care.

Day Five

On the fifth day God creates the wild sea monsters and the birds. At Bethlehem they are represented by their milder counterparts of the sixth day, the ox and the sheep! The wild things know their place. They are outside the stable, in the dark night. We do not know who or where they are in the narrative, only that they are *around*. Perhaps they were present in wind and rain, and what necessitated the overnight shelter. Perhaps they are thieves or prying officials. Perhaps they wear the faces of the obedient Roman soldiers who massacre the innocents at Herod's command. Whatever the wild things are they are never quite to be tamed or trusted, never to be wholly assimilated. Yet they are still God's and he uses them, mysteriously, to guard us and to warn us, in spite of the mischief they can cause us in the conscious world.

The snake is not absent. He reappears in the prophecies that surround the coming of the Saviour in the Christmas story. The curse in the garden of Eden (Gen. 3:14–15) condemns the snake to creep on the ground. There he lies in wait to injure humankind. But the promise is that the snake will eventually be overcome and be crushed under human feet. Some icons and statues of Mary show her with the serpent beneath her feet. Yet I have always noticed that the serpent is far from crushed, but looks remarkably alive and well as it rests under her robes. Shrines where Mary is honoured often fall under the protection of Michael the archangel. It is Michael who defeats Satan and binds him in his proper place, which is the underworld.

In our praying we must learn first to become aware of the inner monsters which are so strange to us. They are not to be wholly tamed. But we must also seek access to the gifts they bring us, the treasures which they guard. Christ harrows hell, and brings up what the devil has imprisoned. And again, Mary has a part in this. A hymn of the Orthodox tradition Church describes Mary as the one who enlightens those who lie in the darkness of death. She is sometimes depicted walking through the shadows of death holding a huge taper, which she is bringing out into the light of day. In some way the dangerous creatures of the inner universe are both toxic and life-giving to us, and it is our task to distinguish them, following in Mary's way. It may fall to us to have to bind the devil. Our task may be simply to acknowledge the wild things and then ignore them. We may find ourselves having first to listen to them with respect and then again listening to them when they grumble and stamp about.

Day Six

On the sixth day God makes the man and woman who together bear the divine image. The Genesis writers write this up and plant a lie in our memory. They say[3] that male man came first, and that woman came from Adam's rib. Yet we all know that every man and woman who has lived on the planet has come from a woman's womb.

God comes to Mary and parts our falsehoods with humility. God shows up the arrogance of male man by being born of a woman who is not submissive to men. Mary the virgin is the friend of women, just as she is the mother of women and men. At Bethlehem creation is restored to its proper shape. The mother and the male child are at the centre of our redemption, and, for once, Joseph, as male man, stands aside, acknowledging powerlessness. Men cannot give birth, and this is the secret of their jealousy and aggression. Mary bears God into the world. The woman rejoices in God her saviour.

So in our praying we need to distinguish the falsehoods and the truths about our sexuality. This includes letting ourselves be the real men and women that we are before God. Most of

[3] In Genesis 2:4ff.

us are neither sexual stereotypes nor sexual neuters. It means believing in the part we have to contribute to the image of God, both in what we need and what we have to give. It also means allowing for the dignity of our differences in the paths we take to come to sexual and spiritual maturity. Jesus and Mary were both unconventional in their sexual choices, especially in a world where heterosexual marriage was even more normative than it is in ours. Yet the Holy Family in its ordinariness and in its tasks does bring affirmation and comfort to those whose first choice must be the creation and care of a human family.

Day Seven

On the seventh day God rested. That rest is also open to us. It is the Sabbath-rest of the people of God, which we are to strive to enter. The way in is by the narrow gate, the low door. This is Bethlehem, the house of the homeless God, the house of bread, the house of healing, where Mary brings Jesus Christ into our helpless world. To Bethlehem the rich and gifted come. Their journey is long and dangerous. Poor shepherds come, and their journey is short and easy, from just over the other side of the hill. So we will search for Bethlehem all our lives. And yet in another sense it is never as far away as we think:

> How far is it to Bethlehem?
> Not very far...